ReBorn
A New Identity

BOLA OLIVIA OGEDENGBE

REBORN A New Identity

Copyright © 2017 Bolanle Ogedengbe

All rights reserved. No part of this publication may be reproduced, stored in a retrieval system, distributed, or transmitted in any form or by any means, including photocopying, recording, or other electronic or mechanical methods, except for brief quotations in printed reviews, without the prior written permission of the publisher.

979-10-95039-05-1 9791095039051

Dépôt légal February 2016

All Scripture quotations, unless otherwise indicated, are taken from *The Holy Bible, New International Version*® NIV®. Copyright © 1973, 1978, 1984 by International Bible Society®. Used by permission.

Printed in the United Kingdom

Dedication

To the ABBA HOUSE church family.

You are an inspiration, and communicating the truths of God's Word to you is one of the great joys of my life.

TABLE *of* CONTENTS

Preface 7

Born Of God 11

Loved Of God Loving God 23

Adopted Into God's Family 33

Forgiven 45

Declared Not Guilty 57

Indwelt By The Holy Spirit 67

Delivered, Invested With Authority 83

Delivered From Sickness 97

Fully Provided For 111

Kingdom Citizen & Ambassador 121

Conclusion 137

Preface

Some twenty years ago, a dear friend made this statement, 'It is a wonderful life in Christ.' I did not understand it because I was not 'in Christ'. Being one of those Christians was, in my opinion, anything, save wonderful. They were an odd bunch. But shortly after, my life was turned upside down by an encounter with Jesus. It became clear to me that His claims were true and I must embrace them, and Him. I did both.

And so began a journey of discovering the richness of this new life, a journey which, in all truth will never end. We are invited to handle divine treasures which too often elude our comprehension. For believers and, in particular, new believers to live free of the shackles of the past and savour to the full their new relationship with God, they must have a good grasp of their new identity. That is why this book was written.

In the book, we explore ten dimensions of this new identity, what happens when we say yes to Jesus. Each chapter includes an exposition of the topic, with practical application and devotional elements. Finally, there are questions and a call to action. Read the book through in one go, but take the chapters one at a time as a daily or even weekly devotional, just to give the information time to sink in. Believe me, it is a wonderful life in Christ. Shalom!

Bola Ogedengbe

Acknowledgements

I wish to acknowledge, thank and honour my Lord Jesus Christ. He met a twenty something young woman heading out on the adventure of life and turned her life right side up. It has been a beautiful divine adventure ever since.

I am grateful to my family for their support, in particular my brother Wale who faithfully reads through every manuscript. I can always count on his involvement in every writing endeavour.

A big thanks to Olive Ncube and Béatrice Lassaigne for their respective contributions. And finally to my church family ABBA HOUSE, thank you for your love and support.

BORN of GOD

Everyone who believes that Jesus is the Christ is born of God, and everyone who loves the father loves his child as well.
1 John 5.1

Figure 1: Return of the Prodigal Son - Rembrandt

1
Born *of* God

One evening, a man came up to Jesus to speak with Him. He was a religious man; a leader of the people with burning issues on his mind. He acknowledged that Jesus was sent by God and he recognized the greatness of His work. Then Jesus looked at him and answered his unspoken question. Jesus stated that to enter the kingdom of God, "You must be born again."

Picture the look of stunned surprise on the man's face. He was a pious man, possibly a good man. He received no accolades, no encouragement whatsoever to continue with his good works which would guarantee his requisite place in the kingdom. Rather, he was confronted with a condition which he obviously failed to meet as he did not even understand it. He was at a loss as to what this could mean, 'A grown man return to his mother's womb?' he asked, 'No, certainly not.'

Jesus proceeded to explain to him the two births that a human must experience to enter the kingdom of God. In so doing, He forever altered our perception of God's relationship with humans. He gave the keys that after His death and resurrection will usher multitudes into the new era, the era of God with man; the era of salvation. What exactly did He say?

We are born twice?

He said that 'what is born of the flesh is flesh, and what is born of the Spirit is spirit' and that Nicodemus should absolutely not be surprised at what He said. So there are two births? Yes, and we need both. First, the birth by which we gained physical entrance into this natural world. That is what Jesus called being born of the flesh. Then there is the second birth by which we gain spiritual entrance into the supernatural world of God. Jesus called it being born of the Spirit. *That is the new birth experience.* It is the work of the Holy Spirit and it is indispensable for salvation.

"I tell you the truth, no-one can enter the kingdom of God unless he is born of water and the Spirit" (John 3.5).

Jesus marveled at Nicodemus because he was a leader of the people and did not understand these things. We want to understand these things. A good understanding of what happened to you when you were born again will stand you in good stead for the rest of your life in Christ.

What exactly happened to you?

The new birth is a spiritual birth; it is the life of God communicated to a person through the Holy Spirit. Why do we need the life of God? Because since the Fall, all humans are dead in sin. Jesus came to the earth, to pay the price for sin, so that all can be forgiven when they come to Him in faith. There are a number of things that happen in us at that point. One of them is that the spiritual death is removed and we come alive. The Holy Spirit makes our spirit alive, and it is no longer separated from God because of sin. It becomes inhabited by the Spirit of God. Thus, our spirit is born again.

You may say, 'If it is so vital for me, I want to be sure that I have received it.' Let us listen to the Scriptures to see how one receives it. One of the closest disciples of Jesus when He was on earth was the apostle John. He wrote, by inspiration of the Holy Spirit, some of the most profound things about Jesus you will ever find. He wrote,

> *"Everyone who believes that Jesus is the Christ is born of God"* (1 John 5.1a)

And also,

> *"But these are written that you may believe that Jesus is the Christ, the Son of God, and that by believing you may have life in his name"* (John 20.31).

Do you see the extraordinary goodness and wisdom of God? John 14.6 is yet another confirmation that the Holy Spirit gives you spiritual birth when you believe that Jesus is the One sent by God to save mankind, when you believe that He is the Son of God.

REBORN

"I am the way and the truth and the life. No-one comes to the Father except through me."

We echo Peter's confession of faith when he said, 'You are the Christ, the Son of the Living God'. So it is by faith in Jesus alone that we are born again. That life is what every man needs, what every man can receive to enter the kingdom of God. That, in a nutshell, is the new birth. That is how we are born of God.

Now, you see that when you believed and prayed to receive Jesus, repenting of your past sins and committing to serve Him with your spirit, soul and body, that is what happened to you. You are now born of God. You are no longer 'dead in your sins'. Your outward appearance may be the same, but make no mistake, you are what the Book calls 'a new creation'. Remember, this is not about outward form, even though you will engage in seemingly religious activities like Bible reading, prayer, evangelism, etc. Rather, it is a giving of life, a supernatural transaction in the spirit realm. It is the act of salvation. What has happened to you? You are saved.

What does this mean?

It means that:

1. Since the life of God is in you, you can have fellowship with God. You have also become more sensitive to His Spirit.
2. You are united with Jesus by the Holy Spirit.

3. You have gone from death to life.
4. You have been transferred from the dominion of darkness into the kingdom of God. You are now a child of light.
5. Your destination is heaven and no longer hell. So, there is also a change in your eternal destination. You will be with God forever. When you die, you will go to heaven to be with God, albeit temporarily. At the end of the age, you will participate in God's plan of creating a new heaven and a new earth.
6. And you will be a part of the reign of God on the earth.

This is radical goodness! It is all yours freely in the new birth, but cost Jesus a great deal. As you continue your life in Jesus, you will meet many classes of people who refuse to accept His offer. Some will say they find it hard to believe because it is just too good to be true, or perhaps simply too good to be true for them because they are very bad people. Conversely, some believe they are too good to need it, and that it is too restrictive. They are convinced that all it takes is for people to do all the good they can and not harm anyone. Nicodemus arguably was a good man, but nevertheless, he needed to be born of God.

> *You are now born of God. You are no longer 'dead in your sins'. Your outward appearance may be the same, but make no mistake- you are what the Book calls 'a new creation'.*

God has blessed you greatly by giving you this new life through the sacrifice of Jesus on the cross. It must remain precious to you. It is the greatest gift anyone can receive. So what do you do with this now?

What do I do?

- **Be grateful.** Begin by thanking God every single day, and several times a day for this new life.
- **Devour the Scriptures.** Consume them as if they were going out of print. Some people will tell you to read a chapter a day; I suggest you read whole books a day. Develop a voracious appetite for God's Word. There is more of this good fare in there. The more you engage with God's Word from the word go, the more fulfilled your life in Christ will be.
- **Enjoy** being saved. Think about it a lot. Take time to read this book over and over again, and marvel at this new life you have received freely.
- **Do not worry** about all that is left to correct in your life. Do not condemn yourself. (See the chapter on forgiveness).
- **Worship God.** Let an endless stream of worship flow from you to God. You do know that you did not deserve any of this, do you not? It is He who is amazing. So tell Him so.

BORN OF GOD

SCRIPTURES TO CHEW ON

John 3.3 "In reply Jesus declared, "I tell you the truth, no-one can see the kingdom of God unless he is born again.""

1 Peter 1.23 "For you have been born again, not of perishable seed, but of imperishable, through the living and enduring word of God."

1 John 5.1 "Everyone who believes that Jesus is the Christ is born of God, and everyone who loves the father loves his child as well."

John 3.16 "For God so loved the world that he gave his one and only Son, that whoever believes in him shall not perish, but have eternal life."

1 John 5.11-12 "And this is the testimony: God has given us eternal life, and this life is in his Son. He who has the Son has life; he who does not have the Son of God does not have life."

John 3.18 "Whoever believes in him is not condemned, but whoever does not believe stands condemned already because he has not believed in the name of God's one and only Son."

Colossians 2.13 "When you were dead in your sins and in the uncircumcision of your sinful nature, God made you alive with Christ. He forgave us all our sins."

2 Corinthians 5.17 "Therefore, if anyone is in Christ, he is a new creation; the old has gone, the new has come!"

PRAYER

Father God, thank You for the new birth I have received in the Lord Jesus. Thank You that Your life is in me now. Thank You for saving me from an eternity in hell and giving me the hope of heaven. Thank You for transferring me into the kingdom of Jesus.

What can I say, Lord? I am blessed beyond imagining. All of this is given to me for free, but cost Jesus dearly. Father, I give You my life to be useful to You, so as to bring others to experience the new birth and be reconciled to God just as I have been.

Bless me, Lord, by making my life useful for Your kingdom. I want to be like Peter, a fisher of men. Teach me, Lord, all that I need to know to take Your Word of salvation to my generation. In Jesus' name I pray, Amen.

Say this continually:

I am born again. I am born of God. I am a new creation. I have been made alive in God. I have eternal life and I will live the rest of my life glorifying God.

QUESTIONS TO PONDER

1. How does one become born again?

2. How can you be certain that you are born again?

3. What difference does this make in your life now?

4. Can you list three things that you ought to begin doing now that you are born again?

LOVED of GOD
and LOVING GOD

We love because he first loved us.

1 John 4.19

Figure 2: Return of the Prodigal Son - James Tissot

2

LOVED OF GOD
LOVING GOD

There was once a young man, much like many young people today, who was impudent, greedy, self-serving and disrespectful. He lived with his father and brother. He suddenly got it into his head one day, whereas his father was still alive, to demand his own share of the inheritance his father would have left him at his death. Yes, quite shocking. What would you have thought or done? Railed at him, called a family meeting to call him to order, or disinherited him for wishing you dead? Any or all of the above would have been my choice. The father, as Jesus told the story, recounted by the gospel writer Luke, acceded to his request, made no effort to force him to stay in the family, and let him go with his inheritance.

The impudent young man travelled abroad to see the sights and indulged in extravagant living. The fool and his gold are soon parted and as was to be expected, it was not long before he found himself in dire straits. Far from God and family, he was reduced to eking out a meagre existence in the most degrading employment imaginable.

Distress, sorrow and near starvation conspired to bring him back to his senses and he decided to return in ignominy and seek forgiveness. He thought perhaps he could beg for a wretched place to lay his head and something to eat, with no hope whatsoever of being reinstated into the family.

He set out for home. As he neared the homestead, the father saw him from afar. Many a parent would prepare the whip, sharpen the tongue and give him the lashing of his lifetime. Not this father. He threw dignity to the wind, hitched up his robe and ran to meet the son and enthusiastically welcomed him home. The son still tried to mouth a few words of repentance, to crave tolerance, but the father cut him off and poured his love out on him. He had him cared for, brought out their very best provision which had been set aside for special occasions. It was a day of rejoicing, not recrimination.

When the older son grew jealous of the attention paid to the erstwhile miscreant, the father gently chided him for not seeing that the brother was lost and was now found. In his love, his focus was not on the wrongs he had suffered at the hands of this wayward son, but on ensuring his well-being now that he had seen the error of his ways. His pain at the son's betrayal was swallowed up by the joy of the son's redemption. We have betrayed God, and when we repent, heaven rejoices.

Lost, found, and loved

Jesus told this story to illustrate the heart of God towards a person who was lost and returns to God. That person is you. You were living a wayward life far from God, acting as your own master, but now you have returned to the 'Shepherd' of your soul. And He is pouring out His love and acceptance on you unstintingly. Many people fear coming to God because they think He cannot love them because of their wickedness. The father in this story could not wait to take his son in his arms. In his eagerness, he ran towards him. What an amazing picture of love.

> *God's love for us is one of the most consistent testimonies of Scripture. It is a deep, unqualified, overriding love whereby He ever seeks to do us good.*

And the greatest good for a human is to be brought back into relationship with God. The love dimension of His nature is so profound that one Scripture puts it this way: 'God is love'. God desires that we return to Him; He welcomes us back unconditionally despite the evil we may have done, as in the story told above. Even more astounding is the fact that it is He Himself who has made it possible for us to be able to come back. When you understand that it was love that made Him give Jesus to die for us, that it was love that caused Jesus to give Himself for us and make it possible for us to come to God, then you can no longer doubt that God loves you.

Perhaps you have not always known that. Many in the world today imagine that because there is so much evil in the world, God must not be good and must not love humanity. Evil is the result of sin and God has shown His love for us in that He made a sacrifice so huge it is mind boggling. He sacrificed His Son to deflect our punishment unto Himself so that our sins can be forgiven. In coming through Jesus, anyone can receive the love of God.

WHAT DOES THIS MEAN?

It means that:

1. You can now receive the love of God. You will find that it is like no human love. You will find that it is unconditional, endless and unfathomable. It is not a generic love; it is personal and targeted, and the target is you, as an individual.
2. One of the most beautiful things about this new life you have received is that not only are you loved by God, you also love God. It is a wonderful thing to love God, to have your affections directed at the Almighty Himself. This is not to be underestimated in the least. It is more valuable than every treasure and all treasures put together. It is a gift of God and a clear demonstration that your heart has been changed by God. Our sinful hearts can love nothing but ungodliness and to love a holy, pure and perfect Being is only possible because His Spirit has given us new life.
3. Loving God enables you to have a beautiful relationship with Him, to enjoy Him and He you. And this love will continue to grow as you spend time with Him in prayer and read His Word. You will become a great admirer of God and a great worshipper.

4. You are finally home, in a relationship with the one Person who knows everything good and bad about you but loves you perfectly. You can be free of rejection, anxiety, fear, and all those things that cause emotional turmoil. You can live in joy, peace and serenity. So go for it.

You can no longer be self-seeking and thinking only of what suits you. You will now be looking for ways to please God.

WHAT DO I DO?

- **Enjoy! Ponder** the fact that you are loved by a pure, amazing, perfect God. Ponder the Scriptures that talk about God's love for you. Do it all the time and just enjoy it.
- **Tell and thank.** Thank God for loving you; exercise that new love you have for God by telling Him how much you love Him. Do this several times a day, as often as it comes to mind. It will transform your relationship with Him and cause your gratitude quotient to shoot through the roof. Your confidence in your new life will also increase and when you happen upon the jeerers and killjoys, your joy in God will overwhelm their jeers and wipe the smirk off their faces.
- **Please Him.** Loving Him also means doing what pleases Him. You can no longer be self-seeking and thinking only of what suits you. You will now be looking for ways to please God. The Bible enjoins us to find out what pleases the Lord, and Jesus said that those who love Him will obey Him.

SCRIPTURES TO CHEW ON

John 3.16 "For God so loved the world that he gave his one and only Son, that whoever believes in him shall not perish but have eternal life."

Romans 5.8 "But God demonstrates his own love for us in this: While we were still sinners, Christ died for us."

Galatians 2.20 "I have been crucified with Christ and I no longer live, but Christ lives in me. The life I live in the body, I live by faith in the Son of God, who loved me and gave himself for me."

Ephesians 2.4-5 "But because of his great love for us, God, who is rich in mercy, made us alive with Christ even when we were dead in transgressions—it is by grace you have been saved."

1 John 4.9-11 "This is how God showed his love among us: He sent his one and only Son into the world that we might live through him. This is love: not that we loved God, but that he loved us and sent his Son as an atoning sacrifice for our sins. Dear friends, since God so loved us, we also ought to love one another."

Matthew 22.37 "Jesus replied: "Love the Lord your God with all your heart and with all your soul and with all your mind."

(1 Peter 1.8; Romans 8.28; 1 John 5.3)

PRAYER

Lord, thank You for loving me. Thank You because Your Word says that You loved us so much that You gave Your only begotten Son so that we can believe in Him and not die but have everlasting life. I do believe in Him, Lord. And because You love me, You call me Your child. Thank You.

Father, I want to love you with all my heart, with all my soul and with all my mind. I know you have already poured your love into my heart and I am very grateful Lord. You are a wonderful Father.

I will love you with my life. I will live in a manner worthy of You. Father, please teach me to honour You as I ought with my life. In Jesus' name I pray, Amen.

Say this continually:

I have come home to my God and I love Him deeply. I belong to God and have been crucified with Christ. I will remain in the house of the Lord all of my life.

QUESTIONS TO PONDER

1. What do we learn from the story of the Prodigal son?

2. Jesus loved you enough to die for you. What do you think of that?

3. How do you show your love for God?

4. If God loves the world, why is there evil in the world?

Adopted *into* God's Family

How great is the love the Father has lavished on us, that we should be called children of God! And that is what we are! The reason the world does not know us is that it did not know him.
1 John 3.1

Figure 3: Return of the Prodigal Son - Esteban Murillo

3
ADOPTED *into* GOD'S FAMILY

It is never wise to take your history lessons from films. As a young person, one of my favourite films was *The Fall of the Roman Empire*. Christopher Plummer's Commodus was a definite attraction, but the main fascination was the character of Marcus Aurelius. In studying history, I discovered later that there was more to him than the film showed, some of it quite unsavoury. I also learnt, hence the mention of him here, that he was an adopted son.

Adoption was a common custom in Roman society and Roman emperors would often adopt their successor. Adoption under Roman law was a complex process. It was also public and enjoyed high esteem. Unlike contemporary adoption, only male adults were adopted, women, rarely, and for good reason. The purpose of adoption was to provide an heir for a paterfamilias in case of lack of male descendants or relations. The adoption process took place in the presence of witnesses, some claim as many as seven. The adoptee lost all rights in his former family, but gained full rights in the new family. His status changed, often going from slave or plebeian to patrician. He became a full heir to all the property of his new father and family, and whatever he owned beforehand came under the jurisdiction of his new father. Whatever prior debts he may have incurred were deemed cancelled as he was now a new person. He became the full possession of his new father under the Roman custom of paterfamilias, where the father exercised total authority over all his children. He also was bound to certain responsibilities in the new family.

To the churches in Rome, in the region of Galatia and in the city and environs of Ephesus steeped as they were in the Roman culture of adoption; the apostle Paul wrote that one of the salient aspects of faith in Christ is that the believer was adopted into God's family. In light of the previous description, picture the impact of these words in Romans 8.15-17,

> *"For you did not receive a spirit that makes you a slave again to fear, but you received the Spirit of sonship. And by him we cry, "Abba, Father." The Spirit himself testifies with our spirit that we are God's children. Now if we are children, then we are heirs– heirs of God and co-heirs with Christ, if indeed we share in his sufferings in order that we may also share in his glory."*

When you came to faith in Christ Jesus, God literally adopted you into His family. You are now able to call Him Father as if you had always been a part of the family. The Holy Spirit witnesses to the fact and makes it a reality for us. Not only that, we become heirs of God. The kingdom becomes our inheritance. So we now share everything with Jesus, we share His sufferings, and we share His glory. What an extraordinary provision! This is hugely significant because many people imagine that whether or not they know Christ, they are children of God anyway, but that is not so. There is a legal transaction that takes place whereby you become a child of God at the new birth.

That is why in the opening lines of the gospel of John, we read that those who received Jesus and believed in Him received the power to become sons of God. Indeed, one of the greatest testimonies of God's love is that we can now be called children of God. A great honour has been conferred on you, do not take it lightly. God now calls you His child, and all because of Jesus.

Jesus is the unique Son of God. And He came to the earth so that we can also become sons of God. Now, do not be thrown by the constant repetition of the word *sons*. It refers to both males and females, but as we saw earlier, usually only males were adopted. Furthermore, even when females were adopted, the males still enjoyed a more prominent status than they did. Thus, the use of the expression *sons of God* further emphasises the special status granted to us in Christ Jesus. Think of this: God has adopted you, so now, Jesus calls you His brother or His sister. It is not blasphemous, it is purely scriptural. Jesus, the Scriptures say, is not ashamed to call us His brethren. To ponder this is to wonder, is it not?

Once, in a Moroccan restaurant, after tucking into a 'tajine aux pruneaux et aux raisins', some of the staff engaged us in a discussion of the Christian faith. They challenged us on the cross; they believed that a prophet could not die on a cross. We explained to them that Jesus did die on the cross and that He was not replaced by a look-alike as they claimed, and told them why. Then they challenged us on the divinity of Christ. We explained why the Bible says that Jesus is the Son of God, and God made flesh and not just a prophet, as Islam claims. (Truth be told, we were used to such questions). We were in a sense accustomed to such objections, but at one point in the course of the discussion, one of them, stunned, exclaimed in shock, "How can you say that you are children of God, God has no children?", whereupon we proceeded to tell them about adoption and being born of God. It made us realise that something which we had almost taken for granted, a great benefit obtained for us by Jesus, the fact that humans can be children of God, was an idea too unfathomable for them.

And indeed, if the Word of God did not state it in such clear terms, we could not begin to imagine that we could ever be called children of God. The Scripture in 1 John rightly exclaims at the wonder of it all, that God would love us with a love so profound that we would be called children of God. Then, the apostle crowns it beautifully, by saying, not that it is what we hope to be, but that it is what we already are. It is not an imposition; it is a true description of our new status, of your new status. And the reason you will find that many people around you do not realise it is explained in this passage. It is because they do not know God, so they do not know His children. But you need to know today that in all truth, you are now His child; He has adopted you into

His family. Whatever your religious background, Jesus, when you came to Him put you in the family of God. So just what kind of Father is God?

What kind of Father is God?

He is the best kind of Father, a Father of incomparable goodness and love. He accepts you unreservedly in Christ Jesus and He loves you completely.

A Father who is faithful, a Father who protects, who liberates His people from bondage, from fear, and from insecurity. He is a Father who makes full provision for His own, and never abandons them.

Jesus emphasised the generosity of God the Father. He taught His disciples to pray to our Father in heaven asking Him to provide their daily bread. He also stated that our heavenly Father gives good things to those who ask Him. Every child of God needs to have a deep understanding of God as their own Father, not simply as the Father of humanity as a whole, but their own Father as well.

WHAT THEN DOES THIS MEAN FOR YOU TODAY?

It means that:

1. At the new birth, you became a new person. Indeed, God's Word says that in Christ you are a new person, that old things have passed away and all things have become new. You have a new status with God and a new nature.

2. Your old moral debts have been cancelled.
3. You are loved, and God accepts you without reservation.
4. You have come into a divine inheritance; you are an heir and co-heir with Jesus to all divine graces.
5. You are free of past rule and dominion.
6. You have come under the full authority and dominion of God.
7. You can enjoy all the privileges of sonship in the kingdom.
8. You are a brother/sister of Jesus.
9. You can enjoy the love of your caring Father.
10. You can now be intimate with the Father and be able to pray with the help of the Holy Spirit.
11. You can trust Him. He will care for you and never abandon you. He said,

> *"Even to your old age and grey hairs I am he, I am he who will sustain you. I have made you and I will carry you; I will sustain you and I will rescue you"* (Isaiah 46.4).

12. You can enjoy the protection of the Father, be totally free of insecurity, bondage and fear and enjoy easy access to God. As the Scriptures say

> *"Let us then approach the throne of grace with confidence, so that we may receive mercy and find grace to help us in our time of need"* (Hebrews 4.16).

13. You can receive spiritual and material provision always. The father of the Prodigal Son said to the older brother, 'Son, all I

have is yours'. God has opened up His resources to you. You will always have help. But God must never be for you merely a means of obtaining help. He must forever be the lover of your soul to whom you offer worship and thanksgiving continually.

What do I do?

- **Think** about it, yes, think about how this changes you and your life. Think about things you believed about yourself that must now change in the light of this new relationship with God. Consider listing them.
- **Thank God** ceaselessly for adopting you. Choose to get to know your heavenly Father by increasing your time spent in His Word and in prayer. And when you pray, ask the Father to reveal Himself to you. Reiterate the fact that you love Him and want to please Him. The prodigal child is home to stay.
- **Commit** to becoming as close to Him as is possible for a human to be, with the help of the Holy Spirit of course.
- **Call Him Daddy**. The Aramaic word, 'Abba' means just that- a familiar form for Father. It may feel strange initially, especially if you are from a background where God was somewhat a distant entity.
- **Change**. Whatever your image of a father is, let God change your thinking so that it will not hinder you from enjoying this beautiful father/child relationship with your heavenly Father. Choose to step into this benefit of salvation.

SCRIPTURES TO CHEW ON

Ephesians 1.4-6 "For he chose us in him before the creation of the world to be holy and blameless in his sight. In love he predestined us to be adopted as his sons through Jesus Christ, in accordance with his pleasure and will— to the praise of his glorious grace, which he has freely given us in the One he loves."

Romans 8.15-17 "For you did not receive a spirit that makes you a slave again to fear, but you received the Spirit of sonship. And by him we cry out, "Abba, Father." The Spirit himself testifies with our spirit that we are God's children. Now if we are children, then we are heirs—heirs of God and co-heirs with Christ, if indeed we share in his sufferings in order that we may also share in his glory."

Galatians 4.5-6 "...to redeem those under the law, that we might receive the full rights of sons. Because you are sons, God sent the Spirit of his Son into our hearts, the Spirit who calls out, "Abba, Father."

Galatians 3.26 "You are all sons of God through faith in Christ Jesus."

John 1.12 "Yet to all who received him, to those who believed in his name, he gave the right to become children of God."

PRAYER

Dear Father, thank You for adopting me into your family. It is a great privilege for which I am grateful. Thank You again for the cross of Jesus, which made this new relationship with You possible.

Now Father, I ask You to help me to know You as I ought to. Reveal Yourself to me in Your Word and in prayer. Teach me Your ways, as You taught Moses, and Paul the apostle, who used to be hostile to Jesus and then became a champion of the faith.

Father, as an obedient child, I submit my whole life to You. Direct me as You will, into what You will, when You will. I acknowledge that You know all things better than I, even my own self. Please give me answers to the questions and circumstances in my life. I am counting on You Father for guidance, instruction and protection, in the name of Jesus, Amen.

Say this continually:

I am adopted into the family of God; I am an obedient child and a credit to God's family. My life will cause many to honour my Father God. He will have pleasure in me eternally.

QUESTIONS TO PONDER

1. What does being adopted by God mean to you?

2. How does it change your vision of God?

3. What is the role of the Holy Spirit?

4. What difference will it make to your lifestyle?

FORGIVEN

For he has rescued us from the dominion of darkness and brought us into the kingdom of the Son he loves, in whom we have redemption, the forgiveness of sins.
Col. 1.13-14

Figure 4: Return of the Prodigal Son - Leonello Spada

4
FORGIVEN

Before Jesus was crucified, Pilate, the governor gave the people the opportunity of securing His release. There was a practice whereby once a year he would release a condemned criminal as a gesture of goodwill. He thus asked the people to choose between Jesus and Barabbas a notorious criminal. He asked the people which of them should he release to them. They chose to have Barabbas released and Jesus put to death. Consequently, Jesus was maltreated and crucified. But he was not to be crucified alone. The rulers had more criminals on hand, and Jesus was crucified between two thieves. One of them persistently nagged Jesus to save Himself and them; the other rebuked his comrade for speaking without fear of God, after all, he said, they both deserved their punishment whereas Jesus was innocent. Then he spoke to Jesus and humbly asked that Jesus remember him when He came into His kingdom. In response, Jesus, in agony and pain, still demonstrating compassion, promised him entry into Paradise that same day. He was forgiven.

And so, in one split second, forgiveness and access to heaven were granted to a man who had lived a life of crime, who had violated all principles of right conduct in society to the point where society had decided they were better off without him. What we learn from this story is the amazing willingness of God to forgive and the fact that Jesus had and still has the power to forgive sins. The man spoke in repentance; he acknowledged he was a sinner and that Jesus was righteous. That is how anyone receives forgiveness from God. People do not like to talk about sin. Have you ever heard anyone complain that religion puts guilt on you, that the problem with religion is that it makes people feel bad?

> *People do not like to talk about sin. Have you ever heard anyone complain that religion puts guilt on you, that the problem with religion is that it makes people feel bad?*

Well, those are people who have not understood that one of the main benefits of knowing Jesus is forgiveness. Like the thief on the cross, you do not have to pay for all the evil you have done, for your indifference or rebellion towards Him in the past. When you commit to follow Jesus, you repent of your sins and evil ways and God in return, in love, forgives you.

That is one of the reasons why Jesus came, so that God will have legal grounds for forgiving us. Can you see how amazing that is? We have sinned, we deserve punishment, legally we must be punished, but God finds a way to get forgiveness across to us. Jesus takes away the punishment that we deserve, so those who come to Him no longer have to face punishment, rather they receive pardon. Furthermore, God does more than forgive, He also removes guilt. That is the answer to give anyone who says religion makes people feel guilty. The truth is that people are already guilty, and as they draw nearer to God, they become more conscious of their guilt. But God wants to free them from it.

Many have misunderstood this story and decided to put off their repentance until just before death. They would spend their lives in sin and disobedience to God and slip into heaven at the last minute. Note that this man had no idea he would be crucified next to Jesus. He could not possibly have imagined such a last minute pardon, which may be why he received it. Those who deliberately postpone repentance may find that the end will come too suddenly for them to repent.

Too easy?

Once, in conversation with a friend who was interested in Christianity, I told him the good news of God's forgiveness in Jesus. His response, 'It is too convenient, in fact too good to be true. You mean,' he said, 'I will be forgiven simply because I believe in Jesus, without me doing anything else?' I said, 'Yes.' He thought 'No, too easy.' That is yet another category of persons. They want you to give them something tough to do to earn forgiveness, like some tough act of penance, but believe in Jesus? No! The problem though is that it is too hard for us, even impossible. There is nothing humanly feasible that we can do to earn forgiveness. It exceeds our scope of possibilities.

God had to do it Himself in Jesus and it was certainly not easy for Him. It was horrific, gruesome and excruciatingly painful. It was spiritual anguish beyond what our minds can fathom. In the garden of Gethsemane as He agonised in prayer before His arrest, He literally sweated blood. He went so far as to ask if this cup could be taken from Him, and He only went through with it because of His submission to the Father. You see there are spiritual dynamics in the Passion, Cross and Resurrection of Jesus that we do not comprehend. It is the measure of God's extreme kindness and love for us that He would put His Son through so much so that we could come to Him without having to pay. Our response should be to receive this free offer of forgiveness with great humility.

So, never take for granted the forgiveness that God offers. Choose to overflow with thanksgiving and joyful expressions of gratitude. Forgiveness is a priceless gift. Many withhold it for feckless reasons and hold vengeance over another's head with glee and sometimes rage. Not so with God. His forgiveness is total, complete and free. It is an encounter with the grace of God. Ephesians, chapter one, verse seven puts it this way,

> "In him we have redemption through his blood, the forgiveness of sins, in accordance with the riches of God's grace."

God is infinitely rich in grace and He has poured forgiveness out in the measure of that richness of grace. It is rich grace of unlimited quantity and quality. Would that I could awaken you to contemplate the unfathomable depths of God's mercy, God's favour, God's goodness and God's grace. I would love to see you celebrating Him without ceasing because of your gratitude for these innumerable spiritual benefits.

The one Person authorized to hold a sword of Damocles over your head has chosen not to. He has chosen to blot out your sins and your transgressions, as stated in Acts chapter three and Isaiah forty three. I think at this point, you are already jumping for joy. If you are not, read this passage again until you catch a powerful glimpse of the overwhelming love of God and of His great sacrifice for you, undeserving though you were.

Do not fall into the trap of self condemnation, rather, forgive yourself and glorify God for His kindness to you. God has forgiven you and He offers you a new beginning.

WHAT DOES THIS MEAN FOR YOU?

It means that:

1. You are forgiven. Whatever you may have done in the past, God has forgiven you and no longer holds it against you.
2. God no longer remembers you did it. Not that He suffers memory loss, but He has chosen to obliterate our past evil conduct and to make us understand how total His forgiveness is, the Bible says that He will no longer remember our sins.
3. Before God, it is as if you have never sinned. You are spotless, at least you were when you came to Christ, if you have committed other sins since, ask Him to forgive you.
4. You do not need to keep reminding yourself of how bad you were. You can also forgive yourself without being presumptuous. You choose to agree with God.

5. You are free to begin again. Every day with God is a new beginning. Seize the opportunity for a fresh start.

What do I do?

- **Thank** the Father for the amazing provision of forgiveness in Jesus. No one else is like God who totally wipes the slate clean. Heap copious and continuous thanks on Him. Never forget how important it is to honour God and show our appreciation. Also, the more you do this, the greater your consciousness of being forgiven and this is very important.
- **Repent.** If God is showing you that you need to do so, repent. You may want to confess specific sins as the Lord lays them on your heart. Confess everything you have done wrong that you remember.
- **Receive forgiveness**. Many times, after coming to Christ, we become more sensitive to God's heart and realise how wrong our previous lifestyle was. Do not torture yourself by dwelling at length on your unsavoury past. Accept that Jesus has paid the price for you to be forgiven. And when thoughts of guilt or condemnation arise unbidden over past sins, you want to avoid the trap of self-condemnation. Instead, heap praise and gratitude on the Lord for forgiving you those very sins. Honour Him by accepting your forgiveness and by ceasing to mull over the past. So, forgive yourself and take time to glorify God for His wonderful kindness to you.

- **Ask God** to redeem the wasted years. Ask Him for a new perspective and direction for your life whereby you can now devote yourself to good works. John Newton was a former slave trader who later came to faith in Jesus. He never forgot his years as a slave trader, but he did not let them stop him from going on to fulfil God's plan for his life. He went on to write hundreds of hymns, became a pastor and famously mentored William Wilberforce, who was successfully used by God in the British Parliament to outlaw the slave trade. He turned his consciousness of the evil of his past ways into a song of praise to God that has traversed the centuries. Some claim the tune may have been that of a West African song sung by slaves on the slave boats. The first lines of his song Amazing Grace read,

'Amazing grace, how sweet the sound,
That saved a wretch like me!
I once was lost but now I am found,
Was blind, but now I see.'

- Finally, **ignore** the mockers. Sometimes people will even accuse and mock you saying, 'Yeah right, after all the sin you have committed, you are now hiding behind the cloak of religion.' Do not allow yourself to doubt God's forgiveness. God, who alone is the true judge will forgive when humans, with our limited understanding of grace continue to distrust, attack and mock.

SCRIPTURES TO CHEW ON

Acts 3.19 "Repent, then and turn to God, so that your sins may be wiped out, that times of refreshing may come from the Lord."

Ephesians 1.7 "In him we have redemption through his blood, the forgiveness of sins, in accordance with the riches of God's grace."

Hebrews 10.17 "Their sins and lawless acts I will remember no more."

Colossians 1.13-14 "For he has rescued us from the dominion of darkness and brought us into the kingdom of the Son he loves, in whom we have redemption, the forgiveness of sins."

Matthew 26.28 "This is my blood of the covenant, which is poured out for many for the forgiveness of sins."

Isaiah 43.25-26 "I, even I, am he who blots out your transgressions, for my own sake, and remembers your sins no more. Review the past for me, let us argue the matter together; state the case for your innocence."

1 John 5.3 "This is love for God: to obey his commands. And his commands are not burdensome."

(Romans 8.1; Isaiah 1.18; Psalm 103.12; Ephesians 4.32; Psalm 51.7, 9)

PRAYER

Father, I ask You to forgive me for all my past transgressions. I have not been obedient to You. From this day forward, I want to please You in all that I do. Thank You Lord for Your forgiveness, thank You that You remove my sins and You choose to forget them. Father, deliver me from all consciousness of guilt with respect to my past, that I may enjoy the full privileges of being forgiven and receive the peace that You give. Thank You for freedom from condemnation and accusation.

I forgive all those who have sinned against me. I choose to hold nothing against them. Heal me, Father of all pain caused by other people's conduct. I forgive even as Christ Jesus has forgiven me.

Thank You Lord that I am free of pain and recriminations. I look forward to a beautiful future in You.

Say this continually:

I was a wretched sinner, now I am gloriously forgiven. God has shown me unqualified mercy in Jesus. I am wholly and completely blessed and committed to honour my King.

QUESTIONS TO PONDER

1. What does the story of the forgiven thief reveal about God?

2. If nothing humanly possible can be done to obtain forgiveness, how then can we be forgiven?

3. What are the steps to receiving forgiveness?

4. How can God forget your sins? A case of memory loss?

Declared
NOT GUILTY

For all have sinned and fall short of the glory of God, and are justified freely by his grace through the redemption that came by Christ Jesus.

Romans 3.23-24

Figure 5: Return of the Prodigal Son - Jan Steen

5
Declared
NOT GUILTY

Jason stands at the bench awaiting sentencing. He has committed the crime, he is guilty; he knows it, the judge knows it, he knows the judge knows it and so all he can do is ask for mercy. The judges return from their deliberation, he stands in terror, thinking his life is about to end. The presiding judge reads out the verdict – *'Not guilty.'*

Jason is stunned. The judge continues, 'We have decided to show mercy. Jason's father has chosen to take the blame for the crime.' Jason cannot get his head round it. His idea of clemency is 5 years rather than 20; at best, some sentencing or other, but he is walking free. And what's more, his criminal record is wiped clean! What is this? He hears the judge again, 'Now, you are to walk in newness of life.'

What happened to Jason? He was 'justified'. When we came to Christ for clemency, God justified us freely. Despite our guilt, He declared us not guilty.

How can this be?

In redemption, Jesus paid the price for humans to be released from the captivity of sin and from the penalty of sin. That price is the reason that, because of the kindness of God, we can be declared just. Since all have sinned, we must have no illusions about how good we are. The best that a human is and does can never merit the goodness of God. God chose to wipe the slate clean and leave you with no criminal record. We are acquitted, all charges are dropped; and our accuser, the devil, has had his nose rubbed in the dust. Keep that in mind, despite all that you have done, God has declared you not guilty.

Furthermore, you have just enjoyed a divine exchange. What happened is that Jesus was made sin so that you can be declared righteous. It therefore means that Jesus carried the weight and penalty of sins He did not commit, so we can be put in a right relationship with God which we do not deserve. All this He did through His death on the cross; that is why you will find here and there in the Scriptures, verses that speak of His blood justifying us. That is what it means. Wonderful, is it not?

Also, He went to the cross as your representative, thus, when He was crucified, it was as if you were crucified. Consequently, His victory over sin is your victory over sin.

> *Jesus carried the weight and penalty of sins he did not commit, so we can be put in a right relationship with God which we do not deserve.*

DECLARED NOT GUILTY

WHAT DOES THIS MEAN?

It means that:

1. It is He who now lives in you and you are able, because of this victory, to no longer be dominated by sin. And so the apostle Paul wrote, *"I have been crucified with Christ and I no longer live, but Christ lives in me" (Galatians 2.20a).*
2. You are not just forgiven, you have also been declared not guilty. The charges against you have been dropped. There is now no need to vilify yourself.
3. You are now free from God's anger. You are accepted into a full and right relationship with Him, and you have been empowered to live free from the dominion of sin. That is your identity today. Today, God holds nothing against you. Walk free.
4. Whatever you have been and done in the past, today, accept that God, in His infinite love and because of His perfect sacrifice in Jesus, has declared you not guilty, acquitted.
5. You need not go around feeling condemned for your past. That is why the Scriptures say that even if our sins are like scarlet, they shall be as white as snow. Furthermore, the Bible says that there is no longer any condemnation for those who are in Christ Jesus, who live by the Spirit of God.

What do I do?

- You guessed it, **thank Him**. Thank Him profusely. Thank Him for Jesus taking your place and taking your punishment. Thank Him for the fact that you have been declared just and treated as if you have never done wrong.
- **Renew.** Begin to work on changing your way of thinking. The Scriptures invite us to 'renew' our minds. It means learning from God's Word to think like God and not like we did before. Change begins in the mind. Do this actively. It is of utmost importance. It means that you take the time to meditate so consistently on God's thinking that your own perspective begins to reflect His.

Stop flirting with sin. Some things you used to do are no longer worthy of you. You are now a new creation

- **Reject thoughts** the devil throws at you. They will come, just say, '*No*'. The devil talks to you, yes, he does. His main tactic is to manipulate you to think ungodly thoughts and then proceed to action.
- **Accept change.** Then, do what the judge in our little simulation told Jason, change your lifestyle. You have been crucified with Christ. You are free. It is important that you choose to live a life that honours God As Paul writes in Ephesians 4.1,

"As a prisoner for the Lord, then, I urge you to live a life worthy of the calling you have received."

- **Stop flirting with sin**. Some things you used to do are no longer worthy of you. You are now a new creation. You probably have some things you would like to keep doing because you think there is nothing wrong with them, after all, you think, you are not hurting anyone…Well, you are. You are hurting yourself. Take God's word for it.
- **Put away** everything that is not pleasing to God. That means taking your cues from God's Word and not from the society. Many things which God calls sin in His Word are today called valid lifestyle choices. Be radical, 'walk in newness of life'. God has never redefined sin to fit any generation. Ours is particularly perverse, be aware of that. Now that your garment has been made clean, choose not to soil it again. If you continue with the same things you have been cleared of, you condemn yourself afresh.
- Finally, **share** this good news. Let people know that God has made a way to declare them not guilty, that He loves them and wants to help them. When they ask why you have changed your lifestyle, tell them it is because God wiped out your sins, gave you a clean garment and you want to keep it clean.

SCRIPTURES TO CHEW ON

Romans 5.1,21 "Therefore, since we have been justified through faith, we have peace with God through our Lord Jesus Christ ... so that, just as sin reigned in death, so also grace might reign through righteousness to bring eternal life through Jesus Christ our Lord."

1 Corinthians 6.11 "And that is what some of you were. But you were washed, you were sanctified, you were justified in the name of the Lord Jesus Christ and by the Spirit of our God."

Romans 8.30 "And those he predestined, he also called; those he called, he also justified; those he justified, he also glorified."

Romans 3.24 "...and are justified freely by his grace through the redemption that came by Christ Jesus."

Romans 6.6,11 "For we know that our old self was crucified with him so that the body of sin might be done away with, that we should no longer be slaves to sin...In the same way, count yourselves dead to sin, but alive to God in Christ Jesus."

1 John 5.3 "This is love for God: to obey his commands. And his commands are not burdensome."

(Romans 12.1-2; 1 Corinthians 6.19; Ephesians 4.4; John 1.29; Romans 6.12-14; 18,19,23; Romans 5.17)

PRAYER

Father, I am not guilty, how wonderful! Thank You for giving me a clean record. You hold nothing against me, thanks to Jesus. What a joy to belong to such a merciful God.

I renounce the devil and his works. I renounce the sin in my mind, my thoughts, my words, my acts, and my body as it does not honour You. Father, strengthen me against temptation. Give me joy in doing Your will. Jesus is my example of holiness and self-denial.

Father, I shall not write new accusations against myself. I choose to honour You with my life, to do only what pleases You. I do not always know why some things please you and others do not. I recognise that I have been conditioned by my society. Help me to share Your values Lord, so I will obey You and change. Teach me Your ways so I may be in symbiosis with You. In the name of Jesus, Amen.

Say this continually:

I am forgiven, free of condemnation and guilt, and I have peace with God. I love holiness, and purity. I am dead to sin, but alive to God in Christ.

QUESTIONS TO PONDER

1. Jesus justified us. What does that mean?

2. Jesus was our Substitute. What does it mean?

3. What does it mean to live a life worthy of your calling?

4. What does 1 John 3.7 say? How will you respond to it?

Indwelt by *the* Holy Spirit

And I will ask the Father, and he will give you another Counsellor to be with you forever-the Spirit of truth. The world cannot accept him, because it neither sees him nor knows him. But you know him, for he lives with you and will be in you.
John 14.16-17

Figure 6: Return of the Prodigal Son - Palma il Giovane

6

Indwelt by The Holy Spirit

May I introduce you to Philip. Philip lives a very privileged life. He is born of God. Not only that, it is obvious that God is always with him, in him, around him; loving him, encouraging him, teaching him, consoling him, directing him, correcting him, empowering him and talking to him every day and every moment! He lives an extraordinary life. Amazing, isn't it?

And someone may be thinking, 'I too could live an extraordinarily beautiful life if I had access to that kind of relationship with God.' Many would not even dream it possible. After all, God has a universe to run, why would He pay so much attention to them? Not everyone can be a Philip. Right? Wrong. Everyone who is born again can live this way.

God has made provision for it by giving every single believer His Holy Spirit. When you commit your life to Jesus, one of the things that happen is that the Holy Spirit gives life to your spirit.

You become inhabited by the Spirit of God and He begins to communicate with you in line with the heart of God. He will do for you what he does for our friend, Philip. How can you be sure of that? Well, you see Jesus made the promise before He left this earth. He promised that the Holy Spirit, (the Paraclete), would be our helper so that we would not be lost and alone in the world; He would come to give us power. Jesus spoke of Him as the One who would come, in John 14.15-17,

> *"If you love me, you will obey what I command. And I will ask the Father, and he will give you another Counsellor to be with you for ever—the Spirit of truth. The world cannot accept him, because it neither sees him nor knows him. But you know him, for he lives with you and will be in you."*

He is not speaking of any other prophet as some strangely and erroneously claim, but of God the Holy Spirit. The Holy Spirit is the third Person of the Trinity, thus a Person who acts, thinks, speaks and expresses volition, not an impersonal force. Understanding this will help you to better follow His direction. The believer is the temple of the Holy Spirit. The Holy Spirit has that special mission to administer the benefits of the cross in the earth and in the lives of believers. He always honours Jesus.

WHAT DOES THIS MEAN?

According to Jesus and God's Word, it means that the Holy Spirit will:

INDWELT BY THE HOLY SPIRIT

1. *Teach* you God's words. You can have the assurance that the Bible will now begin to make sense to you. You see, it was the Holy Spirit who inspired the Scriptures to begin with. That is why the apostle Peter wrote that men wrote as they were moved upon by the Holy Spirit. Now, He is with you and as you read, He will give you understanding. Not everything will be explained on the very first day, but rest assured that things will definitely change from now on.
2. *Show* you God's ways. That is a promise that Jesus gave us about the Holy Spirit. He opens a window into the doings and thoughts of God and breaks it down for us. Too often we see God as inscrutable, but He is anything but. He has taken a lot of trouble to get us to understand Him to some extent so we can relate with Him.
3. *Comfort* you. Yes, He will comfort you. He brings peace in pain and healing in distress. He will often bring Scripture verses to mind that will be a great comfort to you.
4. *Encourage* you. He will sustain you in those times when doubts assail and temptation is strong to give up on God's plan for you. Or perhaps you are tired of your continuing efforts yielding no results. From now on, the Encourager is with you.
5. *Guide* you. The Spirit knows the mind of the Father and will show you the direction to take in life and what to think, say or do. As you follow Him, your life will naturally fulfil divine purpose.

6. *Strengthen* you. Do you ever feel as if you have used up every ounce of strength left and you cannot take it anymore, or you do not have any more energy to accomplish a task? Well, God supplies strength through His Spirit. He will make you mighty inside and outside. God is strong, yes, strong and He likes His children to be strong and able to face any situation or circumstance head on without capitulating. The Bible has numerous references to God strengthening His people.
7. *Stand by to help* in any way required. The journey of life frequently calls for assistance and reinforcement and the wonderful Holy Spirit repeatedly comes to our aid.
8. *Help you to pray.* Indeed, one of the ways in which the Holy Spirit comes to our aid is by helping us to pray. The book of Romans, in a very interesting passage reveals the believer's inadequacy in prayer and the role of the Holy Spirit. His assistance is supernatural, not through words that are intelligible to us. He helps us to pray because He knows the mind of God, and so we are able to pray the real issues in the right way.
9. *Empower you to witness* - I find it remarkable that when Jesus was going to leave the earth, the very last conversation He had with His disciples had to do with the Holy Spirit giving them power to witness for Him. And on the day that they received the Holy Spirit, the power to witness was immediately put to action, and it was amazing. We

receive power to witness also when we receive the Holy Spirit.

10. *Work miracles.* Yes, He does, even today. Some will endeavour to discount miracles today, but they are wrong. The Holy Spirit has not been deprived of one of His prerogatives, the working of miracles. So in receiving the Holy Spirit, begin to believe that He will work miracles for and through you.

11. *Testify that you are God's child.* Absolutely beautiful. God's provision is all encompassing. The Scriptures say that the Holy Spirit communicates to our spirit that we are children of God. Nobody can beat that out of you, you are God's child. If you are not sure that you are saved, ask the Holy Spirit to show you your true condition, and He will, because He is the same One who convicts the world of sin. So either He will convict you of sin or He will testify that you are God's child. Either way, doubt no more.

All said and done, what all this basically means is that He will make your life a roaring success. You will know what you need to know, do what you ought to do, in the strength and ability that God gives. Your primary objective now that you are in Christ should be to know God through His Word and prayer, and to know His will and direction for your life. And all these precisely are the focus of the Holy Spirit's actions in the earth and in you. Jesus said, pay attention to this, that He will take the things of God the Father and of Jesus and communicate and show them to us.

You wonder if you can be sure that He will do all this for you. Yes, He will. As it is, He has already done a lot for and in you. In fact, He is the One who made you aware you needed Jesus; He touched your heart and made you aware of your sinful condition. That is why you responded and gave your life to Jesus. He was outside, now He has moved inside you. And from now on, He will continue the work He has started. Yes, He will do all these things for you.

When Jesus speaks of the other Comforter to come, He is not speaking of any other prophet coming after Him, but of God the Holy Spirit, who did indeed come on the day of Pentecost.

God has set you up for a good life. What is a good life? A life lived in full agreement with the plans and desires of God. Do you see that? Now that you have His Spirit, you can train yourself to live in agreement with God because you have access to His mind. I know that sounds extraordinary and it is, but it is also true. Are you beginning to see the new birth for what it is, a divine innovation of monumental proportions?

How can you be sure you received Him? You do not feel any different? Well, because Jesus promised that God would give the Holy Spirit to those who ask Him. The Bible is categorical in affirming that believers are the temple of the Holy Spirit, which means that every believer has the Holy Spirit.

This of course means that we are no longer our own, we belong to God and as the Holy Spirit directs our lives, we are to honour

Him with our conduct. 1 Corinthians 6.18-20 reads thus:

> *"Flee from sexual immorality. All other sins a man commits are outside his body, but he who sins sexually, sins against his own body. Do you not know that your body is a temple of the Holy Spirit, who is in you, whom you have received from God? You are not your own; you were bought at a price. Therefore honour God with your body."*

The Baptism of the Holy Spirit

Now let's take this a step further. Every believer receives the Holy Spirit indwelling him at the new birth. But we see that there is a subsequent experience with the Holy Spirit when He fills a believer and overwhelms him that Scripture refers to as being baptised in the Spirit, i.e. immersed. Usually, this is accompanied by the ability to speak an unknown language.

God enables you to speak to Him in a language you did not learn, a language that He causes to flow out of your spirit under the influence of the Holy Spirit. This is a spiritual communication that bypasses the human mind. It does not replace the Word of God; it is one of the powerful ways that God helps His people to live victoriously and supernaturally in the world. You build yourself up spiritually when you pray in tongues, you speak mysteries to God, pray the perfect will of God.

If you have not experienced it before, you may think it strange when you see people speaking in tongues. However, it is no stranger than going into a room where everyone is speaking

Yoruba and you do not understand a word of what they are saying. It is yet another beautiful example of God's great love for you, and of His desire to help you live a powerful life in Him.

So, now that you have access to the baptism of the Holy Spirit, to prayer in unlearnt languages; you also have access to the gifts of the Holy Spirit. The gifts? Yes, the gifts or more precisely, the manifestations of the Holy Spirit. Simply put, the Holy Spirit does supernatural things through God's people. For instance, He will release power to heal a sick person, He will release power to bring about a miracle, He will give information supernaturally about a situation or person of which the person giving the information had no prior knowledge. He will show what kind of spirits are operating in a situation, whether it is the Spirit of God or evil spirits, etc.

Spiritual and supernatural

Remember, God is spiritual and supernatural. So, welcome to a world of supernatural events. When we cooperate with the Holy Spirit, He will work in us, for us and through us. So you are a recipient of God's goodness, but also a carrier of God's goodness to other people.

That is the amazing potential you now have as a believer. Rejoice that God makes such superhuman provision available for His children. Change your way of thinking and receive the baptism of the Holy Spirit yourself. Step into a new and exciting life in the Spirit.

INDWELT BY THE HOLY SPIRIT

WHAT DO I DO?

- **Shout for joy** to begin with. Have you ever heard news this good before? Your life has been turned into a thing of beauty and potential awesomeness. No, it is no exaggeration, underline these words and you will read them again with great conviction in a short while. In fact, if I could break into song in writing this, I would. Yes, shout for joy because what God has done for you in giving you the Holy Spirit to accompany you in your Christian life is beyond price.
- **Be grateful** to God for the Holy Spirit.
- **Pray** to become more sensitive to Him and to His guidance in your life.
- **Spend time meditating** on Scriptures about the Holy Spirit so that you can be in tune with what God's Word says concerning Him. Let me warn you, you will run into some very nice, very godly Christians who are firmly convinced that the Holy Spirit does not do supernatural things anymore. They believe He does not empower people to speak in tongues or do miracles anymore. Do not let them confuse you, they are wrong.
- **Ask for prayer** that you may be baptised in the Holy Spirit.
- **Pray in tongues** every day. Honestly, why would you deprive yourself of the untold benefits of praying perfectly, accurately, according to the heart of God, and praying

even for things you do not know about, because the Holy Spirit helps you to pray?
- **Honour the Holy Spirit** by living a pure life.

Isn't it remarkable that the last conversation Jesus had with His disciples on the earth had to do with the Holy Spirit?

INDWELT BY THE HOLY SPIRIT

SCRIPTURES TO CHEW ON

John 14.15-17,26 "If you love me, you will obey what I command. And I will ask the Father, and he will give you another Counsellor to be with you for ever - the Spirit of truth...But the Counsellor, the Holy Spirit, whom the Father will send in my name, will teach you all things and will remind you of everything I have said to you."

John 16.12-15 "I have much more to say to you, more than you can now bear. But when he, the Spirit of truth, comes, he will guide you into all truth. He will not speak on his own; he will speak only what he hears, and he will tell you what is yet to come. He will bring glory to me by taking from what is mine and making it known to you. All that belongs to the Father is mine. That is why I said that the Spirit will take from what is mine and make it known to you."

Romans 8.26 "In the same way, the Spirit helps us in our weakness. We do not know what we ought to pray for, but the Spirit himself intercedes for us with groans that words cannot express."

1 Corinthians 3.16-17 "Don't you know that you yourselves are God's temple and that God's Spirit lives in you? If anyone destroys God's temple, God will destroy him; for God's temple is sacred, and you are that temple."

(Luke 11.13; 1 Corinthians 6.19; Romans 8.14-17; Acts 2.38; Acts 1.8)

PRAYER

My dear Father, there are no words to describe Your goodness. You made provision for me to be saved through the Lord Jesus. And you made provision for me to live for You through the Holy Spirit and Your written Word. Thank You my Father. Thank You for the Holy Spirit who is in me. I honour Him, recognise and acknowledge His presence in my life. I submit to You to be led by Your Spirit, help me to be sensitive to Him, so that I can live in a manner worthy of You.

Father, propel me into the dimension of the supernatural, work miracles through my life by Your Spirit.

I want to be baptised in the Holy Spirit, I desire the ability to speak in other tongues and declare mysteries to God.

Thank You Father for all this goodness. In Jesus' name, Amen.

Say this continually:

I have the Spirit of the Living God, therefore, I can pray, I can know the mind of God, I can witness, I can see miracles. And because I am His temple, I turn away from sin.

QUESTIONS TO PONDER

1. Who is the Holy Spirit?

2. What role does He play in my life after I am born again?

3. My body is the temple of the Holy Spirit. How should that affect my conduct?

4. What are the benefits of praying in tongues?

Delivered
Invested with
Authority

And having disarmed the powers and authorities, he made a public spectacle of them, triumphing over them by the cross.

Colossians 2.15

Figure 7: Return of the Prodigal Son - Cornelis Massijs

7

Delivered, Invested with AUTHORITY

Let me tell you a story. By the way, if you thought you had read good news up to this point, then prepare to be amazed yet again by God. One day, in my room at university, a friend came to see me. She launched into a conversation on religion, God, Jesus, the necessity that I be born again, etc. Now, I grew up in an Anglican family and had no salvation experience but did not realise it. I had flirted with faith, with atheism, and sundry forms of spirituality. Jesus was not on my radar. Yet, I had not infrequent discussions with Christians, as they were quite persistent in seeking converts. I found the practice abhorrent and would always try to put them down whenever possible.

Well, on this particular occasion, this friend tried very hard to communicate the gospel to me. She was not getting very far and then she compounded matters by talking about the devil and demons. I immediately retorted with disdain that Christians were just as superstitious as the practitioners of diverse African traditional religions, whom they had the temerity to consider heathen. However, I did note, and said as much to her, that though Christians superstitiously believed in evil spirits like the others, they had a different perspective. Indeed, they affirmed that they had the authority to expel demons and that the demons would obey them when they spoke in the name of Jesus. The other side, however, lived in craven fear of those fiends and sought to appease them with offerings. That conversation stayed with me and it is one I often recount when I talk about the authority of the believer and his deliverance from the powers of darkness.

There are many today who think the way I did. You may be just like I was and you are wondering if any of this is for real. On the other hand, you may be different. You may already know first-hand that there are powers of darkness that we must contend with. The truth of the matter is, and this I discovered to my amazement, the devil is real and does oppress people in the world today. Human responsibility cannot be denied, but humans are strongly influenced and sometimes compelled by the devil to do evil; and do themselves suffer evil.

The Bible makes it clear that the devil is the adversary who opposes people's lives. He has opposed you since you were born. 1 Peter 5. 8 says,

> *"Be self-controlled and alert. Your enemy the devil prowls around like a roaring lion looking for someone to devour."*

DELIVERED, INVESTED WITH AUTHORITY

The language is strong. It shows the utter destructiveness and viciousness of Satan. We have to contend with a sophisticated command structure of spiritual forces of darkness. And they use different means of attack - temptation to sin, oppression, possession, sickness, etc. Jesus had to contend with them when He was on earth. Evil is very real and we must not downplay it. Rather, we must rout it wherever we encounter it.

Demons may gain access to people through occult activity, divination, abuse, trauma, injury, and various other means. They can cause compulsive and irrational behaviour, blasphemous and all forms of horrendous thoughts, as well as extreme hostility towards the Word of God. They can also cause physical sickness, horrific dreams, sexual perversions, depression, feelings of hostility towards God Himself, and trigger supernatural occurrences. The list is endless.

However, the tide turned when Jesus defeated the devil on the cross, and succeeded in his avowed intention of destroying the works of the devil. Then, He rose from the dead and ascended into heaven taking a position of complete victory at the right hand of the Father, seated in authority having 'taken captivity captive'. We are told that He is seated far above every principality, power, and name that is named. So all demonic forces are totally, irrevocably and forever subject to Him. The Scriptures add that every believer is in like position as Jesus; seated spiritually in the heavenly places. Ephesians 2.6 says,

REBORN

"And God raised us up with Christ, and seated us with him in the heavenly realms in Christ Jesus."

Consequently, any believer in Christ can resist the devil and he has to obey. In fact, the Bible says he will run far away. He can compel the devil to leave him alone or to leave another person alone who genuinely seeks their help. And you will find that you will need to do this on a fairly regular basis. Why? Because the devil is persistent and does not like to give up. He knows he is defeated, but he also knows that many believers do not know it and have espoused a 'demon less' theology.

We cannot begin to even fathom the depths of evil that exist. That is why the Holy Spirit through the apostle Paul warns us most solemnly to be sober, vigilant and prayerful. He makes it clear in the book of Ephesians, chapter 6 that we do have to contend with the powers, principalities and wicked spirits in the heavens. Jesus won the victory over them through His death and resurrection. However, they are still able to attack those who are not in Christ or those who are in Christ but are careless about their inheritance. That must not be you.

WHAT DOES THIS MEAN FOR YOU?

It means that:

1. Because of Jesus' victory, the devil has lost every right to attack you and the ability to compel you to sin.
2. You can be free of every demonic influence, even if you have practiced occultism, witchcraft, divination, done tarot

reading, séances, astrology and any other such practice. The minute you committed your life to Jesus, the power of God was made available to bring you freedom.
3. You can be healed of any sickness caused by demons. You can be free of every oppression, compulsion and distortion in your life.
4. Every area of your life where the devil has caused havoc can be restored.
5. You have authority over the devil and when you command him to leave you alone, he must. James 4.7 says,

"Submit yourselves, then, to God. Resist the devil, and he will flee from you."

6. Now, that is good news. Watch the progression, you submit yourself to God first, then you say no to the devil. The natural consequence is - he runs away from you.

Satan has lost every right to oppress you. You have gained full rights to stop his attacks every time. If you will boldly stand up to him and rebuke him, he is compelled to leave you alone.

The spiritual world

As you commence your walk with God, it is important that you understand that the spiritual world is real and that you make a clear decision to stay in God's realm and not venture into the devil's realm. In God's realm, you have protection, assurance,

REBORN

victory and authority. Jesus called the devil 'the thief' and said he came to kill, steal and destroy, whereas Jesus has come to give life. He has given you life.

WHAT DO YOU DO?

- First, **rejoice**. There are millions of people in the world who are terrified of the devil, but you have been set free.
- Then, **repent** of all sin. Sin is a safe sanctuary for Satan. He is at home in the life of the sinning believer. Repent in particular of all occult involvement and sexual perversions.
- **Renounce the devil** and all his works. Bear in mind that even if you have not consciously participated in occult activities, it is still important to renounce the devil and take a clear stand. Normal, average people like you and I have been oppressed by the devil for centuries.
- **Renounce specific occult involvement.** In other words, give them up and sever all connections with the spiritual forces behind them. If you have been involved in any form of occult activity, lodges, astrology, necromancy, card reading, etc., you will be happy to know that you can now give them up and enjoy a peaceful life in Jesus. If you yourself have been a medium, you must renounce connection with those spirits or they will utterly poison your existence as you try to walk with Jesus. Light and darkness cannot mix. You must give it up.

- **Get rid of occult objects** in your possession, if any. On one occasion, the apostle Paul went to preach in the city of Ephesus, a place where the people were well versed in the occult. Many people came to the knowledge of Christ and as they did, do you know what they did? They brought out their occult paraphernalia and had them publicly burnt, incurring financial losses but gaining priceless spiritual advancement. So when you renounce these things, remember to destroy the related objects, no matter how valuable, no, do not give them to your neighbour.
- **Ask for prayer** if you are conscious of any kind of oppression such as continuous nightmares, strange occurrences in your sleep, continuous depressive feelings, thoughts of terror, violence, irrational urges to harm yourself or others, unexplained symptoms, strange terrors, etc. Jesus has made the provision for you to be free, totally and gloriously free.
- **Live a life of holiness**; do not open any more doors to the devil by violating the laws of God. Keep your freedom and enjoy it. Sin is a safe sanctuary for Satan. He is at home in the life of the sinning believer. Even if temporarily dislodged, he will return.
- **Affirm your authority**. Now you can take authority over any spirit that tries to oppress you. Command them to leave you alone and they will go. They have to, because of your alliance with Jesus; they are legally bound to obey you. If there is nothing in your life that is an open door

for them, they will have to go. Do not consider yourself, consider Jesus. It is His name that they fear, not your own. Command them to stop their manoeuvres against your life and they will be compelled to obey. Welcome to a life of freedom. Our God is so good. Pray the prayer at the end of this chapter; continue to worship the Lord and you will see His grace released over your life in greater measure.

SCRIPTURES TO CHEW ON

Mark 16.15-18 "He said to them, "Go into all the world and preach the good news to all creation. Whoever believes and is baptised will be saved, but whoever does not believe will be condemned. And these signs will accompany those who believe: In my name they will drive out demons; they will speak in new tongues; they will pick up snakes with their hands; and when they drink deadly poison, it will not hurt them at all; they will place their hands on sick people, and they will get well."

Luke 10.19 "I have given you authority to trample on snakes and scorpions and to overcome all the power of the enemy; nothing will harm you."

Ephesians 6.12 "For our struggle is not against flesh and blood, but against the rulers, against the authorities, against the powers of this dark world and against the spiritual forces of evil in the heavenly realms."

Colossians 2.15 "And having disarmed the powers and authorities, he made a public spectacle of them, triumphing over them by the cross."

1 John 3.8 "He who does what is sinful is of the devil, because the devil has been sinning from the beginning. The reason the Son of God appeared was to destroy the devil's work."

(James 4.7; 1 John 4.4; 1 Peter 5.8-9)

PRAYER

My wonderful Father, thank You yet again for this great salvation. Thank You for destroying the works of the devil through the Lord Jesus. According to Your Word, I am to submit to You, and when I resist the devil, he will flee.

Father today, I submit to You wholeheartedly, spirit, soul and body. I repent of all sin, I renounce it. I renounce the devil and all his works. I renounce all forms of occult activity, I renounce (be specific). And I ask You Lord to remove every trace or deposit of darkness in my life. Let Your power overwhelm me to bring total deliverance.

I cancel every agreement with darkness, and destroy all its works in my life. Satan I resist you, let go of my life. I command every spirit of darkness operating in my life, leave, in the name of Jesus. Thank You Father that affliction departs from my life, and I am free, in the name of Jesus, Amen.

> ***Say this continually:***
>
> Jesus won the victory for me on the cross. So I am free of the dominion of Satan. I am free of every wicked and evil spirit. My life is a demon free zone.

QUESTIONS TO PONDER

1. In what way does the cross affect my dealings with the devil?

2. How do demons gain access to people and what do they do?

3. What is the significance of James 4.7?

4. Why does holiness matter?

Delivered from
SICKNESS

When evening came, many who were demon-possessed were brought to him, and he drove out the spirits with a word and healed all the sick. This was to fulfil what was spoken through the prophet Isaiah: "He took up our infirmities and carried our diseases."

Matthew 8.16-17

Figure 8: Return of the Prodigal Son - Rembrandt

8

Delivered from SICKNESS

And you thought the good news was over! There is more, much more. The people in Jesus' day got a glimpse of it, but it was after His death and resurrection that they came to grasp the awesomeness of this aspect of the work of Jesus. Hear this. One day, Jesus, on leaving the synagogue went with His disciples to the house of one of His apostles, Peter. There they found Peter's mother- in- law confined to bed with a fever. On hearing of it, Jesus went to her and He ministered to her with love and compassion. He touched her, commanded the fever to leave her and she was healed on the spot. We know she was, indeed she got up right away and served them food. Well, the story does not end there. You see, good news travels fast. At the end of the Sabbath, Jesus had to deal with the massive influx of the townspeople. They had heard about the healing and they brought all their sick to receive their share of this unexpected good fortune. Jesus obliged them and the Scriptures tell us that he placed His hands on every single one of them and healed them of sickness and affliction caused by demons.

There are some meetings you would give anything to attend, this is definitely one of them; the joy in the town must have been palpable. Who had ever heard of such a thing? And could it ever happen again? Probably not, we would say, yet we are told otherwise. This remarkable occurrence, we are told, marks the fulfilment of the promise made concerning the Messiah through Isaiah the prophet hundreds of years earlier. According to Isaiah, Jesus would bring healing of sickness and disease as part of His work of redemption. And those who lived in His day were experiencing it even in advance of the cross. How much more should we experience it after the cross and resurrection?

God has always healed; it is part of His nature to heal. Do you know that God has names? I know, you probably thought His name was God. Well, one of God's names is Jehovah Rophe - the Lord who heals. His names reflect His personality. He consistently promised good health to His people if they would obey Him. It is thus unchangeable as it is fundamental to His being. The story of God's people throughout the Old Testament demonstrated this fact. Unlike ritual laws that change from the Old to the New Testament, healing as the expressed will of God to bless His people remains the same. The patriarchs lived to a ripe old age; He brought His people out of Egypt in excellent health, and never stopped providing restoration when they called on Him.

He promised that if they would be obedient, He would bless their food and take away sickness from their midst. Psalm 103 speaks of remembering the goodness of God as He forgives all your sins and heals all your diseases. Disobedience brings sickness. It is not, however the sole cause of sickness as we live in a broken world where evil dominates. The important thing is that God desires His people to be well. Look at Jesus. Jesus is the expression of the perfect will of the Father and His ministry was summarised in these terms by the apostle Peter, that He went about doing good and healing all that were oppressed of the devil.

On that day in Capernaum, He did a lot of good. Healing is God doing good. Jesus demonstrated it, and everywhere He went sick people were brought to Him so He could heal them. Then He sent His apostles out to preach the gospel and also heal the sick and deliver people from demons, which they did.

Healing is God doing good. And everywhere that Jesus went He did good and healed all the oppressed.

Healing is the expression of the will of God. When they asked Jesus if He willed to heal, He said, "I am willing." When they suggested 'if you can' He retorted, "All things are possible to him who believes." He could and He willed. And the remarkable thing is that He empowers His people to be as the apostles were, agents of good and of healing. Before He left the earth, He made it very clear that His disciples, us, would do the same works He did and even greater ones.

So healing did not stop with the Old Testament, it continued with Jesus and it did not stop with Jesus, it continued with the apostles. We see it in the book of Acts. Once the disciples had received power through the Holy Spirit, they began to heal the sick and preach with boldness. In fact, at one point, people brought sick people from all over and were even content to just lay them on the ground so that Peter's shadow would fall on them. The healings were so dramatic and amazing that they had no doubt the people would be healed just by Peter's shadow falling on them. Once, as Peter and John were going to the temple, they happened upon a poor fellow who was lame from birth. He was being carried to the temple where he would sit at the temple gates to beg alms of the incoming worshippers. Interestingly the gate was called 'Beautiful'. Something beautiful was about to happen, but he did not know it yet.

He had no thought of being healed, he just wanted some money. So when he saw the apostles, he turned to them and asked them for money. They, inspired by the Holy Spirit, turned to him and offered him something more than money. They offered him health. Listen to Peter's words. They have much to teach us - "What I have I give you; In the name of Jesus Christ of Nazareth, walk." He said he would give the lame man what he had and proceeded to give him healing. Quite, quite extraordinary! It turned the whole community upside down. Everyone wanted to know how this happened, they all knew the man and could not fathom how he came to be walking. It gave Peter and John a platform to talk about Jesus.

Nor did healing stop with the apostles, it continues with us. When Jesus was leaving the earth after the resurrection, He spoke as the gospel of Mark tells it, of signs that would follow those who believe. And healing was one of them. Besides, since the power did not belong to the apostles, it belonged and still belongs to the Holy Spirit, He can still deploy it today, and He does.

God healed for reasons that are still valid today. He healed out of love, because He had compassion for the people. He healed to meet the need of people. He healed to prove that Jesus was the Saviour; and He still needs to do so today. The effects will be the same, many will believe, some will scoff, some will be amazed, and God will be glorified. Matthew 15. 29-31 says,

> *"Jesus left there and went along the Sea of Galilee. Then he went up on a mountainside and sat down. Great crowds came to him, bringing the lame, the blind, the crippled, the mute, and many others, and laid them at his feet; and he healed them. The people were amazed when they saw the mute speaking, the crippled made well, the lame walking, and the blind seeing. And they praised the God of Israel."*

WHAT DOES THIS MEAN?

It means that:

1. God wants you well. Whatever the reason for you or people you know being sick, do not assume it is God's doing. There are many things going on in the world that God is not responsible for. Sickness is one of them.

2. You can be healed because when Jesus went to the cross, He not only took away your sins, but your sicknesses as well. That is the point that Isaiah was making when he said in Isaiah 53.4-5,

   "Surely he took up our infirmities and carried our sorrows, yet we considered him stricken by God, smitten by him, and afflicted. But he was pierced for our transgressions, he was crushed for our iniquities; the punishment that brought us peace was upon him, and by his wounds we are healed."

3. Healing is total. Expect to be healed also of emotional wounds, trauma and distress of diverse sorts. God cares for the total being. Often, we neglect these emotional pains and focus only on the physical. Yet they are often the cause of many physical ailments.
4. God wants to heal through you. Now that is exciting. We are partners with God in doing His will on earth. Think how thrilling it will be to see God restore people to good health after you pray. You can begin to pray for sick people around you. You do not need a special diploma in 'healing arts' to do so. Of course it is important to learn as much as possible, but God does not require us to be long standing Christians before He hears us.

What do I do?

- As in every other situation, I will invite you to **thank God** profusely for this immense benefit of the new birth and

to do it every day. Thank Him warmly and extravagantly because sickness is a horrendous yoke to bear.
- **Ask the Holy Spirit** to guide you to receive your healing, to show you anything you need to know about your health and follow His directions.
- **Study**. Healing requires revelation, so soak yourself in the Scriptures that speak of God's desire and plan to heal and keep you in good health. Meditate on them, think of them, pray them, and ask the Holy Spirit to give you understanding. Train yourself to speak in agreement with the Scriptures rather than repeat other people's negative comments about your condition. If you do not need healing, indeed you may have already experienced healing in your body; perhaps God even used it to open your heart to the gospel, what then? Well, take time to study the Scriptures on healing so that you can know what God says and be strengthened in your faith.
- **Forgive** any who have offended you. Many times in praying for the sick or those oppressed by a demon, we have found them receive their healing after forgiving someone. Do not live with bitterness. It can make you sick or hinder your healing. You are enjoined to 'forgive as Christ forgave you.' (Ephesians 4.32; Colossians 3.13).
- **Stay out** of destructive arguments about healing. And there are many to be had with persons who have chosen a cautious or even sceptical approach. Healing is a grace to be received not a doctrine to fight over, and you will find

that many in the body of Christ are bent on making it a point of contention rather than a source of blessing. Why lose a potential benefit by listening to those who have chosen not to believe in it? Besides, it is far easier for God to heal your body than it was for Him to save your soul. And He has already saved your soul.

- **Ask for prayer.** Go to people who believe that God wants to heal you and who will stand with you. Seek prayer and support from people who believe that God heals today.
- **Pray** a simple prayer of faith and begin to decree healing in your body. Command the sickness to leave you. Command any spirit attacking your body to go.
- **Praise.** God's power is released when His people praise Him and great deliverance occurs. Praise is also an expression of trust. So when we are at our wits end, when medical science fails us, when we hear that what ails us is incurable, we still do not despair. We praise God. We say, like the psalmist *'I shall not die, but live, and declare the praise of the Lord'*. It comes from Psalm 118. Read the entire psalm, as it describes God's deliverance in an extreme situation. Choose to trust in Him and apply the other principles enumerated above. And when your healing manifests, go crazy with praise; well, in a manner of speaking.
- **Be patient.** Sometimes we need to stay with it until change comes. Not all healing is instantaneous, it is often gradual. As the symptoms recede, testify and praise. Continue in faith and in the word of God.

- **Pray for the sick.** What you want is for this amazing revelation to become a permanent blessing of God for your life and through you for others. Remember, Jesus said that those who believe will lay hands on the sick and they will recover. Sometimes you pray for sick people and they recover when you yourself are still sick. Don't give up, if God is able to heal through you, He is able to heal you.

Healing is a benefit that we have not yet fully understood or utilized. We are all growing in knowledge so that we can see total healing all the time when we pray for people. Love, compassion and a non-judgmental approach, are essential in helping people regain health. Jesus embodied all that and we must imitate Him.

What about medication?

Taking medication does not disqualify you from receiving healing from God. And when you are healed, you will want to have it confirmed by your doctor. He is bound to see it. The important thing is to understand that there is something beyond medical ability.

I stand with you in faith and declare that the power of sickness is destroyed over your life in the name of Jesus. You shall live a life of rejoicing and victory as symptom after symptom falls off you and the divine life of God transforms your mind and body, in the name of Jesus, Amen.

SCRIPTURES TO CHEW ON

Isaiah 53.4-5 "Surely he took up our infirmities and carried our sorrows, yet we considered him stricken by God, smitten by him, and afflicted. But he was pierced for our transgressions, he was crushed for our iniquities; the punishment that brought us peace was upon him, and by his wounds we are healed."

Matthew 8.16-17 "When evening came, many who were demon-possessed were brought to him, and he drove out the spirits with a word and healed all the sick. This was to fulfil what was spoken through the prophet Isaiah: "'He took up our infirmities and carried our diseases.'"

1 Peter 2.24 "He himself bore our sins in his body on the tree, so that we might die to sins and live for righteousness; by his wounds you have been healed."

Exodus 23.25 "Worship the LORD your God, and his blessing will be on your food and water. I will take away sickness from among you."

James 5.14-16 "Is any one of you sick? He should call the elders of the church to pray over him and anoint him with oil in the name of the Lord. And the prayer offered in faith will make the sick person well; the Lord will raise him up. If he has sinned, he will be forgiven. Therefore, confess your sins to each other and pray for each other so that you may be healed."

PRAYER

Father God, I come before You as a beneficiary of grace and I seek healing in my body. I repent of all wrongdoing and I forgive all who have sinned against me and release myself from the bondage of unforgiveness. I receive healing in my soul and renounce all toxic emotions. Lord, manifest Your glory in my body. Lord Jesus, Your Word says that You carried my sicknesses and took away my diseases, that by the stripes that wounded You, I was healed and made whole. So I refuse to carry these sicknesses in my body.

Sickness, in the name of Jesus, I command you to leave my body. Symptoms, physical, emotional and spiritual, be destroyed and evacuated from my life now. I counter every demonic activity; spirits of infirmity, leave, in the name of Jesus. I receive total health in my body and my soul and thank You Lord for all Your wonderful provision for my life. In the mighty name of Jesus I pray, Amen.

Say this continually:

By the stripes that wounded Jesus, I was healed and made whole, so I live in good health. My mind and body are renewed daily and I walk in divine strength.

QUESTIONS TO PONDER

1. Explore the connection between Isaiah's prophecy and the glorious events of that day in Capernaum.

2. God is Jehovah Rophe? What does that show about Him?

3. Why is it necessary to study healing in God's Word?

4. Acts 10.38. Jesus healed all that were under the power of the devil. Do demons cause sickness? If so, what do you do?

fully **provided** *for*

If you, then, though you are evil, know how to give good gifts to your children, how much more will your Father in heaven give good gifts to those who ask him!

Matthew 7.11

Figure 9: Return of the Prodigal Son - Pietro Faccini

9
Fully provided *for*

One day, Jesus looked at the crowd before Him and His heart went out to them. He knew they were bound to be hungry and there was nothing for them to eat. They had been with Him for several days in a remote place listening with rapt attention as He taught them. He also knew His team did not bring enough provisions to feed them. Yet He felt He could not send them home without food. They were likely to faint from sheer hunger before reaching the next town. So, He called His disciples and presented the problem to them. They were at a loss as to how to feed so many people. The logistics of it was mind boggling. What could they possibly do? But Jesus had a way out. They were to bring Him whatever food they could find. They brought seven loaves of bread and a few small fish. A paltry offering.

But it was enough for Jesus. He had the people sit down, took the available food, presented it to the Father and gave thanks. He then had it shared out among the people and as they did, there was more, and more, and more until everyone had eaten their fill. Then they gathered the leftovers, seven baskets in all, many times the initial investment of seven loaves and a few small fish. It was not until then that Jesus sent them on their way. Love and compassion had been satisfied.

This remarkable story was not and is not told for entertainment purposes. Like all Jesus' miracles, it outlines an essential dimension of the character of God and His relationship with His children. This is God loving, caring and making provision for the natural needs of people. Oh, by the way, on that day four thousand people were fully nourished by that paltry initial offering. It is a tale of provision, a window into God's loving heart. It is a statement of intent, a demonstration of faithfulness. This is God, unfazed, undaunted by the most impossible circumstance, able to use whatever He finds to bring about a desired end. This is God, mighty, always victorious. No human circumstance, desperate though it be, can resist the application of His power. It is this power that He unleashes on behalf of His own.

Jesus told us to ask the Father to provide for us because He knows that He can and will do it.

Born again believers now have a Father in heaven, One who, like Jesus in this story, is compassionate. One who knows, and intends to meet the needs of His own children even before they ask. Jesus taught His disciples to address God as Father, and to ask Him, quite boldly, "Give us this day our daily bread." It stands to reason that He wants to, and can, provide their daily bread; why else would Jesus tell His disciples to ask Him?

On another occasion, Jesus said, "Ask and you shall receive, seek and you shall find, knock and the door shall be opened." Can God's children expect His provision in their material life? Absolutely. Paul understood this well. He had seen God provide for his own needs throughout his ministry even when he was not working with his hands as he put it. He wrote to the church in Philippi, thanking them for supporting him financially even though he had learnt to be content with little when he had little. He reassured them that because of their generosity towards him, they themselves would never know lack. He made this stirring statement:

> "...my God will meet all your needs according to His glorious riches in Christ Jesus" (Philippians 4.19).

Think of the story we saw earlier in this book, that of the Lost or Prodigal Son. There is another character in this story whose interaction with the father is indeed most instructive, the older son. When the older son got wind of the celebrations laid out to welcome the errant sibling home, he was deeply upset. He complained to the father that the wayward, unworthy spendthrift was being feted in grand pomp while he, the faithful, obedient son had never been given the least treat despite his unstinting loyalty. The father responded by telling him that everything he the father had already belonged to this son. In other words, he could have had that treat had he thought to ask, had he realised his father wanted him to have it. His father would not have denied him, but he did not know.

We need to know God as our Father and as our Provider. Do you want to hear another name? Jehovah Jireh is one of the ways in which God revealed Himself to Israel and it means the Lord the Provider. So, intrinsic to the nature of God is meeting the needs of His people. Jesus who is the perfect expression of God expressly states that God's people are not to worry about material things such as food, clothes and shoes, as their Father in heaven already knows that they need these things. And then He goes on to say, and oh, how so rich, that if they will focus rather on the things of God's kingdom, all their needs would be provided for abundantly. Do you see how generous God is?

What does this mean?

It means:

1. You can go ahead and shout for joy, God wants to provide for you.
2. God already knows everything that you need, Jesus said so. God even knows what you have not yet asked for.
3. God has already promised in His Word to make full provision for your life.
4. You can stop worrying about the future and about material things. Remember that Jesus specifically told us that it is those who have no God who worry about such things.

5. Obedience to God is imperative for provision. God gives specific instructions about giving, about handling money and about managing our lives. You cannot ignore them and still expect Him to provide.
6. If you will do what Jesus says, all your needs will be met. It is a shame to see what evil people resort to so as to have their needs met. God says, follow me, and I will take care of you.
7. Your generosity will bless others and yourself as well. The book of James shows us that some do not receive from God because of their selfishness. The only reason they ask for anything is to spend on themselves exclusively. That is not good company to be in. We should seek to be generous.

What do I do?

- **Thank** the Lord and praise Him for His great and kind heart. Thank Him that He is such a giver.
- **Focus**. Do what Jesus says; focus your attention on His kingdom, His Word, His truth and on living in holiness.
- **Meditate** continually on His Word so your heart will be settled on this great promise.
- **Be generous**. Honour God and honour people with what you have.
- **Ask,** believe He heard you and what you asked for is yours.
- Keep **thanking** Him for it. In fact, thank Him all the time in all circumstances.
- **Enjoy** being God's child.

SCRIPTURES TO CHEW ON

Philippians 4.19 "And my God will meet all your needs according to his glorious riches in Christ Jesus."

Matthew 6.26, 31-33 "Look at the birds of the air; they do not sow or reap or store away in barns, and yet your heavenly Father feeds them. Are you not much more valuable than they?...So do not worry, saying, 'What shall we eat?' or 'What shall we drink?' or 'What shall we wear?' For the pagans run after all these things, and your heavenly Father knows that you need them. But seek first his kingdom and his righteousness, and all these things will be given to you as well."

Psalms 34.10 "The lions may grow weak and hungry, but those who seek the LORD lack no good thing."

Malachi 3.10 "'Bring the whole tithe into the storehouse, that there may be food in my house. Test me in this,' says the LORD Almighty, 'and see if I will not throw open the floodgates of heaven and pour out so much blessing, that you will not have room enough for it.'" (Deuteronomy 29.5; 1 Chronicles 29.16.)

Hebrews 13.5 "Keep your lives free from the love of money and be content with what you have, because God has said, 'Never will I leave you; never will I forsake you.'"

2 Corinthians 9.8 "And God is able to make all grace abound to you, so that in all things at all times, having all that you need, you will abound in every good work." (Psalm 81.10; Philippians 4.6)

PRAYER

Father, thank You for all that You are and all that You do for me. I marvel that You will take such good care of Your children. Your Word says that I will lack no good thing, thank You. Your Word says that you will meet all my needs, thank You Lord. Father, today I present my requests to You in accordance with Your promise, I ask......... (fill in the blanks). I believe that You have heard me, and it is done. Thank You Lord, In Jesus' name.

Father, I also ask that You will give me understanding of Your commitment to provide for me. I desire that my decisions never be based on money, but always on Your Word. Teach me by Your Spirit what Your Word says about financial, material and life's provision. I want to be blessed, and I also want to bless. According to 2 Corinthians 9.8-11, I will have a full supply and abound in every good work. I promise to honour You with my tithes and offerings. I believe that you will honour me in return. Thank You Father. Amen.

Say this continually:

God is my provider, so I am fully provided for. I am a tither and a giver, free of lack and despair. I receive more than full supply from the Lord so I can be generous.

QUESTIONS TO PONDER

1. What do you take away from the way Jesus fed the crowd?

2. Why, in your opinion, would God meet your needs?

3. Why did Jesus say we are not to worry about food, clothing etc?

4. What did He say to do instead and why?

kingdom citizen, **AMBASSADOR**

For the kingdom of God is not a matter of eating and drinking, but of righteousness, peace, and joy in the Holy Spirit. Romans 14.17

"We are therefore Christ's ambassadors, as though God were making his appeal through us. We implore you on Christ's behalf: Be reconciled to God." 2 Corinthians 5.20

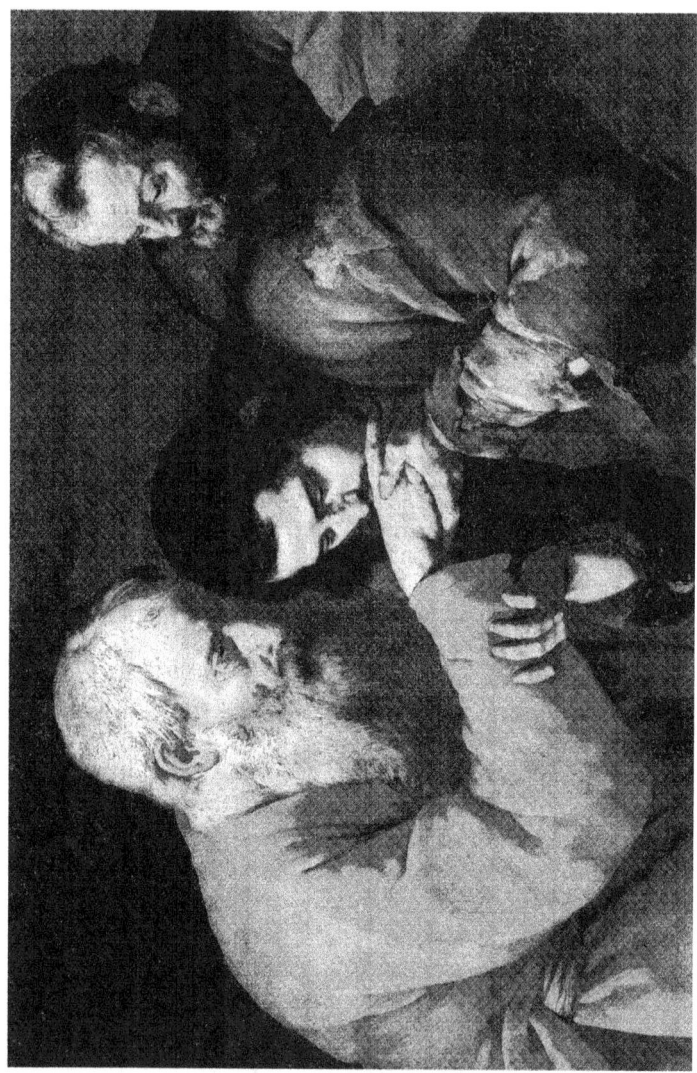

Figure 10: Return of the Prodigal Son - John Warwick Smith

10
Kingdom Citizen & Ambassador

For generations, God's people waited through the many vicissitudes of their existence for 'the' day. They waited for the day that would radically alter their circumstances, and usher in the glorious reign of their God, delivering them from servitude and bringing peace and justice. Messianic expectations and the reign of God came to exist together. A long way from the revered patriarchs, from the glorious days of powerful monarchies, here they were living as vassals to a foreign, pagan power following centuries of toil, hardship, pain, exile, distress and disillusionment. They held on to the hope.

And one day, a shaggy haired, oddly clothed young man, a prophet, found refuge in the desert, thundering to all that the long awaited kingdom of God was at hand; hope was kindled afresh. Was something afoot? They came from far and wide, trooped to him at the River Jordan and testified that their hearts were ready for the reign and dominion of their God. In the midst of these, one day came Jesus. John testified that He was the Lamb of God who would take away the sins of the world. Was that how the kingdom would come?

Far and near Jesus went, teaching, preaching, proclaiming that the kingdom had come; the kingdom had come? Yes, His very presence, His actions, His words, His demonstrations of dominion over sin, sickness, the brokenness of human existence represented the manifestation of the kingdom and the beginning of the fulfilment of the promise of the kingdom. A new era had begun, an era of the reign of God, the dominion of God, and it began with His ministry and subsequent death and resurrection, which opened the way for others to enter the kingdom through repentance and faith in Jesus.

Matthew 4.17 says,

> *"From that time on Jesus began to preach, 'Repent, for the kingdom of heaven is near.'"*

The value of the kingdom

Jesus told a few stories to illustrate a few facts about the kingdom. Once a person was walking along and happened upon a magnificent treasure in a field. On seeing the treasure, the man took it and hid it in the field. Then he proceeded to sell all his possessions to purchase the field and keep the treasure for himself.

Then there was another individual, a merchant who sold fine pearls. Well, one day he came across the most exquisite pearl of all and in order to acquire it, he went and sold all that he owned, and then he took the money and went and purchased that one single pearl. The kingdom of God is that treasure, that pearl that is so infinitely precious that we will exchange everything else that we own for it. Neither of these individuals hesitated, they recognised the value of their find and divested themselves of all earthly prerogatives to acquire it. We can do no less for the kingdom of God.

> *It is better to enter the kingdom maimed and blind in one eye than to go able bodied into hell- Jesus*

There is yet one vital point that you need to know about the kingdom. Jesus illustrated it this way. He said, wait for it, that if your right hand causes you to sin, you should cut it off, if your right leg causes you to sin, you should cut it off and then, if your right eye causes you to sin, you should gouge it out. Now, that does not sound like the Jesus we read about in the secular press, does it? Then he said you are much better off entering the kingdom of God with one hand, one leg and one eye than to go to hell with all limbs and members intact.

Now before you sever your limbs, let me explain. The point Jesus is making is that, as we said earlier, the kingdom is of primary value; therefore your salvation is something to be greatly cherished so much so that you must be radical in disposing of anything that stands in its way, even those things that are themselves very dear to us and even intrinsic to us. Compare that to the attitude of many today who allow even the most insignificant things of life to hinder their commitment to God. Thus, inheriting the kingdom is non-negotiable and no habit, plan, purpose, relationship, occupation can take precedence over it or even diminish our zeal for it.

Life under God

The kingdom of God or of heaven as it says in Matthew is the rule and the reign of God; it is that place, that realm where God rules as king. It is also those who are the subjects of that dominion. Jesus taught His disciples to pray, "Your kingdom come, your will be done on earth as it is in heaven." That is the kingdom. When we believe in Christ, we are born again and ushered into the kingdom. We become those in whom and through whom the will of God will be done, those who are subject to the rule and authority of God. We enter another world spiritually, known as the 'kingdom of the Son he loves'. This means that we must now focus our attention on the ways of the kingdom and our lives must reflect the kingdom. We undergo a process of transformation produced by the renewal of the mind and the power of the Holy Spirit. This is how we become able citizens and representatives of the kingdom, citizens who enjoy the benefits of the kingdom and fulfil the responsibilities of the kingdom.

There is one further qualification of the kingdom that I want to leave with you, and it is this, that the kingdom of God is righteousness, peace and joy in the Holy Spirit. This is going to be your lot from now on as you continue your walk with God. In previous chapters, we emphasised the fact that now you are at peace with God. God holds nothing against you and in fact is rather happy with you because you have committed your life to His Son. He has declared you righteous because Jesus gave you His righteousness. Then think of the joy that is now available to you in Jesus. God loves for His people to be joyful, it is part of the work that the Holy Spirit does in us. I smile as I write this because exchanging our sinfulness for His righteousness is the best deal you can ever get. Enjoy it.

Ambassadors

All of this is good, but would be somewhat limited if we did not grasp the fact that He has not only made us citizens of the kingdom but also its ambassadors. What then is an ambassador? An ambassador, according to Webster's dictionary is the highest ranking person representing his country while living in another. It is also more generally an authorized representative or messenger. It is a person on a mission to bring to bear in another nation the values, principles and policies of his own nation. An ambassador, it goes without saying must be a credit to his country and work for the interests of his home country.

Paul, in 2 Corinthians 5 makes the point that believers are ambassadors of Christ, representing and speaking for Him in the earth. Verse 20 reads,

> "We are therefore Christ's ambassadors, as though God were making his appeal through us. We implore you on Christ's behalf: Be reconciled to God."

The implication is huge. As a believer thus, you have a special status in the earth. You are in the world, but you belong to another realm; you are the citizen of a kingdom whose ways are radically different from those of the world you inhabit. You are called to represent Christ, bring people to know Him, think like Him, espouse His values and basically change their allegiance from Satan to Christ. Why Satan? Because the whole world lies under the dominion of the devil. That is a Scripture by the way.

So, a believer is a person on a mission to change the world for Jesus; that is what defines him.

You have been entrusted with the responsibility of connecting others to God, of reconciling people to God as you have been reconciled.

WHAT DOES THIS MEAN?

It means that;

1. You have been freed from the domination of Satan and are now under the rule of God.
2. Because of this, you must devote your life to finding out what God wants and doing it. You are invited to set your heart on the things that are 'above'. There is a change of focus; the things of God must now captivate you completely.
3. You do not belong to yourself, you belong to God. Consequently, let God direct your decisions from now on, you will find out that He does a very good job of guiding

our lives. You will avoid many disasters by listening for divine direction.
4. You have entered a world of astounding spiritual privileges, one, as the Scripture says, of righteousness (you are considered just by God), peace and joy.
5. You have received all you need for life and piety. You have full provision of every spiritual requirement to live a powerful and beautiful life.
6. You must be totally steeped in the culture of the kingdom of God. In God's eyes, that is where you belong now. So, it should not be an alien entity to you. Rather, you will be so in touch with its values that you live by them with ease and refuse to be drawn into the ways of the country of residence, planet earth.
7. You are an official representative of Christ on earth, you are mandated to speak in His name and bring others to be reconciled to Him as you have been reconciled. The Lord, as Paul puts it, makes His appeal through you. And your cry to them is, 'Be reconciled to God'.
8. Since you are an ambassador of the kingdom of God, your lifestyle must be worthy of God, and you must be one who works for the interests of God's kingdom and His church on the earth. Put away habits and plans that cause you to be unfruitful for God.
9. You become a partner with Jesus in building the church on the earth and making the good news of the kingdom

known in your sphere of influence. You become God's choice instrument to make His name famous in your entourage. Welcome to a life of relevance.

What do I do?

You guessed it!

- **Praise God** with great joy! It is an unqualified privilege to be a child of the kingdom, to be on God's side, under God's rule, to be delivered from under the boot of Satan. You have been transferred from the dominion of Satan to the kingdom of the Son of His love. Think about that.
- **Think.** Consider and measure the great value of this new life in Jesus. As a person who is originally from a country other than the one that is now my home, I have over the years seen the desperate lengths that many people go to in order to acquire citizenship in another country. The acquisition of that citizenship totally changes their lives, their future perspectives and practically their whole existence. No longer subject to the varying constraints imposed on foreigners, they breathe 'new life', travel at will, and a new confidence emanates from them. Think of the freedom in the realm of the spirit, the liberation from fear, torment; think of the new passport you now carry handed over to you without toil, through the sacrifice of another.
- **Willingly submit your life** to the dominion of God. Pray and tell God as often as you think of it that He is welcome

to do whatever He wants in your life, that you will follow Him as He desires.
- **Read His Word** every day, meditate on it, and seek to find out as much as you can about this great King so you can of your own volition agree with Him.
- **Obey God's word.** Yes, obey, not resist, argue, complain; all that is but a waste of time and is most unprofitable. Often, beginning our walk with Christ, we may cherish notions of knowing better than what God says in His Word, though the same, sad to say, still afflicts many old saints. However, it is an erroneous notion. God does know best, as the old saying goes. Think of it this way, you who were a wayward wretched sinner, were saved by an all knowing Being who had made provision for it even while you remained ignorant of your need. Left to you, you would have directed your life on a straight course to eternal damnation. Mercifully, it was not left to you, Jesus arrested your attention and now, here you are, born again. It seems to me that God has proven His utter superiority with respect to yourself, and so, it is wisdom itself to begin the Christian life by acknowledging that and pledging yourself to a life of obedience.
- **Ask God to help you** to represent His message with your words and your life as you ought. For some, the immediate response is, 'Oh no, my life is a mess, I cannot', but they are wrong. We are all a mess when we come to Jesus, for some it is more glaring than for others, but you see

one of the privileges of the kingdom is that you now have the Holy Spirit who will, according to Jesus, guide you, instruct you, help you, sustain you, teach you. So you see, all it takes is that you accept to be helped and you are on your way to being an amazing ambassador of the kingdom of God.

Is it that simple? As a matter of fact, it is.

Will there be challenges? Absolutely!

Will you overcome if you trust the Holy Spirit and obey the Word of God? Absolutely!

If the Holy Spirit was able to raise Jesus from the dead, He can transform your life.

Welcome to a life of great grace.

SCRIPTURES TO CHEW ON

John 3.3-7 "In reply Jesus declared, 'I tell you the truth, no one can see the kingdom of God unless he is born again.' 'How can a man be born when he is old?' Nicodemus asked. 'Surely he cannot enter a second time into his mother's womb to be born!' Jesus answered, 'I tell you the truth, no-one can enter the kingdom of God unless he is born of water and the Spirit. Flesh gives birth to flesh, but the Spirit gives birth to spirit.'"

Matthew 4.23 "Jesus went throughout Galilee, teaching in their synagogues, preaching the good news of the kingdom, and healing every disease and sickness among the people."

2 Corinthians 5.20 "We are therefore Christ's ambassadors, as though God were making his appeal through us. We implore you on Christ's behalf: Be reconciled to God."

Matthew 6.31-33 "So do not worry, saying, 'What shall we eat?' or 'What shall we drink?' or 'What shall we wear?' For the pagans run after all these things, and your heavenly Father knows that you need them. But seek first his kingdom and his righteousness, and all these things will be given to you as well."

1 Corinthians 6.9 "Do you not know that the wicked will not inherit the kingdom of God? Do not be deceived: Neither the sexually immoral, nor idolaters, nor adulterers, nor male prostitutes nor homosexual offenders."

(Matt.5.3; 6.10; 7.21; Luke 17.20-21; Rev. 21.1-4; John 18.36)

PRAYER

Father, I attest to the fact that, as Your Word says, You raise people up from the dung heap; You have brought me out of darkness and established me in the kingdom of the Son of Your love. I am full of gratitude my Lord.

Father, I ask that You open my eyes to understand the value of the kingdom, I want to honour the things of God and give them pride of place in my life.

I refuse all hindrances and weights that encumber and keep me from going full steam for You. Here I am, Lord, send me. Make me a worthy ambassador of the Kingdom. I will be a soul winner. And I will be faithful to You all my life.

Say this continually:

I am a citizen and an ambassador of the kingdom of God.
I enjoy full rights and privileges in the kingdom.
I represent Jesus on the earth and draw many to Him.

QUESTIONS TO PONDER

1. What is the lifestyle of a citizen of the kingdom of God?

2. What are the prerogatives of a citizen of the kingdom?

3. You are an ambassador for God. What does that mean?

4. What is the meaning and rationale of seeking first the kingdom?

Conclusion

But you are a chosen people, a royal priesthood, a holy nation, a people belonging to God, that you may declare the praises of him who called you out of darkness into his wonderful light. Once you were not a people, but now you are the people of God; once you had not received mercy, but now you have received mercy.

1 Peter 2.9-10

Surely, there is no end to the goodness of our God. What an inconceivable work of grace He has accomplished! Needless to say, despite all that has been written in this volume, we have only scratched the surface of the new identity of the believer, as revealed in God's Word.

As you study the Scriptures, you will discover so much more than we can put in a book such as this. We all come to this with our own story, and when we are first born again, do not yet see the full picture of this beautiful work of God. We have stuff that we need to deal with, questions begging for answers, the baggage we need to be divested of, just stuff. A process has begun, a process that will bring these beautiful truths into gradual expression. If you have been practicing the *'What do I do'* section, you are already well on the way.

Remember, life in the kingdom is partnering with God for the fulfilment of His purposes in you, for you, and especially through you for His kingdom's sake. If you will embrace the requisite spiritual disciplines as a lifestyle, you will be unstoppable in enjoying and manifesting the life of the kingdom of God.

I will encourage you to pick up my other book on the new lifestyle of the believer. There I outline ingredients of a new lifestyle, specific actions and steps that will consolidate you in the faith and make you a true ambassador of the gospel of Christ. Embrace them, not as a duty, but as the means by which your life will undergo a total transformation, thus enabling you to accomplish the purpose of God for you on planet earth.

Shalom!

Say this continually:

I am of a chosen race, a royal priesthood, one of God's people, a holy temple, a citizen of heaven, God's workmanship, a minister of reconciliation, a member of the body of Christ.

ABOUT THE AUTHOR

BOLA OGEDENGBE is a lover of God. She is founding pastor of Abba House Church in Paris, France and heads the prophetic ministry 'The Theophilus Company' (La Compagnie Théophile). She speaks five languages and after more than two decades travelling the world as a Conference Interpreter, she moved into full-time ministry and has never looked back.

Her consuming desire is to cover the nations with the gospel. She is a dynamic prophetic minister, teacher, preacher and conference speaker. Her weekly television programme "Passion pour Dieu" reaches a global audience. She is a gifted blogger and writer with several books published and in pre-publication.

Author's blogs

www.bolaoged.com (English)
www.oliviaoged.com (French)
(Subscribe for updates and ebooks)

For ministry, television information

www.compagnietheophile.org (prophetic ministry, conferences, television, etc)
www.abba-house.org (church)

Living for eternity

We must live with an eye to eternity and the principles we apply to our lives today will shape our present and our future.

AN EYE TO THE CROWN covers ten things you need to do to live a victorious life and win the ultimate prize. these principles will inspire, encourage and empower you for a beautiful lifestyle.

30 days to transformation.

REBORN comes with a companion workbook/devotional in 7, 15 and 30 day formats.

It includes quotes, prayers, journal, questions, etc. It can be a stand alone resource but it is best used alongside the book..

www.ingramcontent.com/pod-product-compliance
Lightning Source LLC
LaVergne TN
LVHW012249070526
838201LV00107B/310/J